Nägelein

Designing for Interaction on Mobile Devices

AF189933

Series: Electronic Commerce & Digital Markets
Volume: 8
Editor: Prof. Dr. Martin Spann
ISSN: 2199-7608

Ludwig-Maximilians-Universität München
Munich School of Management
Institute of Electronic Commerce and Digital Markets
Geschwister-Scholl-Platz 1
80539 Munich
Germany
www.ecm.bwl.lmu.de

Philipp Nägelein

Designing for
Interaction on Mobile Devices

Foreword by Martin Spann

BoD – Books on Demand Verlag

Imprint

Bibliographic information is published by Deutsche Nationalbibliothek.
The Deutsche Nationalbibliothek lists this publication in the Deutsche Nationalbibliografie;
detailed bibliographic data are available on the internet at http://dnb.d-nb.de.

Author:
Dr. oec. publ. Philipp Nägelein
E-Mail: philipp.naegelein@gmail.com

Production and Publishing:
BoD – Books on Demand, Norderstedt
In de Tarpen 42
22848 Norderstedt
Germany
E-Mail: info@bod.de
Internet: www.bod.de

Dissertation 2018
LMU Munich/Ludwig-Maximilians-Universität München
Reference Number/Kennziffer: D 19
Foreword by Prof. Dr. Martin Spann

1st Edition 2018

Cover design & layout: Dr. Philipp Nägelein
Cover image: © Thawatchai Kurunun / iStockphoto.com

Printed on FSC-certified paper.

ISSN 2199-7608
ISBN   978-3-7460-0757-1

Foreword

The optimal design of the digital interface to the customer is one of the key success factors in electronic commerce. An online seller's digital interface is responsible for its product presentation as well as the interaction between the company and its customers. Several scientific disciplines have studied the interface design: From a marketing perspective, it relates to the sales channel and the product presentation, from a computer science perspective it relates to questions of the so-called "human computer interaction" and from a psychology perspective to questions of product perception. For an online seller, an optimal design of the digital interface to the customer is the primary goal to increase product sales and profits.

The proliferation of mobile devices (e.g., smartphones and tablets) has created new opportunities and challenges for the design of the digital interface to the customer. Mobile devices differ from desktop or laptop computers in that they are controlled by so-called touchscreens rather than a computer mouse or touchpad. In addition, mobile devices are highly personalized devices that users usually carry with them anytime and anywhere. Interaction via touchscreens on a highly personalized device can substantially affect the perceived attractiveness of products as well as product purchases, which must be taken into account when designing websites for mobile devices.

The goal of Philipp Nägelein's dissertation is the analysis of three types of factors influencing the user interaction with mobile devices: Product-related, interface-related and consumer-related factors, which he derives in his first interdisciplinary literature-based study and subsequently analyzes in three empirical studies.

In his empirical studies including large-scale field and online experiments, Philipp Nägelein demonstrates that different navigational control mechanisms such as the direction of navigation (scrolling vs. swiping) and the amount of information provided can have a significant impact on consumer choice. Further, he identifies important moderators such as the textural fit between the surfaces of products and touchscreens.

Philipp Nägelein's dissertation provides important theoretical insights into consumer behavior affected by the digital interface as well as the digital device. Further, his results are of high practical importance for online sellers as well as website developers. I wish that research and practice in marketing and human-computer interaction will benefit from the insights of this dissertation.

Munich, February, 2018   Martin Spann

Acknowledgements

Holding this – or any – dissertation booklet in the hands, one might get the impression that more or less all of the work inside can be attributed to a single person, the author. This perception, however, is widely mistaken. Much rather, a large number of remarkable people contributed in many different ways.

First of all, I would like to thank my advisor Martin Spann. With your feedback and advice, your mentorship and guidance, your patience and trust, you inspired me far beyond academic research. In a similar way, I would like to express my gratitude to my second advisor Thomas Hess and in particular to my further co-authors Florian Lachner, Andreas Butz, and Robert Kowalski. Building bridges between the disciplines of management, marketing, and human-computer interaction has been a fruitful and rewarding challenge.

Day in, day out, my colleagues at the CDTM management team were there for me through all the ups and downs along the road: Laura Bechthold, Gesa Biermann, Patrick Bilic, Patrick Christ, Michael Chromik, Fabian Dany, Maximilian Engelken, Florian Gall, Veronika Gamper, Claudius Jablonka, Florian Korte, Florian Lachner, Kilian Moser, Stefan Nothelfer, Benedikt Römer, Julian Sußmann, and Stefanie Weniger. Thank you so much for your continuous support, advice, and friendship.

Furthermore, I would like to thank my colleagues at the Institute for Electronic Commerce and Digital Markets: Daniela Baum, Gábor Darvasi, Stefan Daurer, Andrea Dechant, Andreas Heusler, Lena Hoeck, Chinmay Kakatkar, Katharina Maßner, Dominik Molitor, David Prakash, Lucas Stich and Kamilla Zab. Even though we did not share the same office every day, you've always made me feel like a part of your ECM family and supported me not only with my research, but also as true friends.

Uta Weber at CDTM and Waltraud Broch at ECM deserve a special mention. Whenever I arrived at your place, you would welcome me with a smile, with the latest news, and many times with delicious food.

Sebastian Schuon and Max Müller supported me in the realization of my research, involving a time commitment far beyond anything I could have ever asked for. Simon Eumes, Pascal Fritzen and Florian Fincke developed state-of-the-art mobile interfaces to conduct user studies online. Coye Cheshire and Jeff Burton provided me with the opportunity to spend three months as a visiting researcher at UC Berkeley. A large part of my research has been financed through the Software Campus research grant, with ongoing mentoring and support by Verlagsgruppe Georg von Holtzbrinck, namely by Christian Gerlich, Annegret Teichert, and Volker Smid.

Last but not least, I would like to thank my family and close friends, who I can always count on. Your permanent love and support means everything to me.

Munich, February, 2018   Philipp Nägelein

Table of Contents

I   Introduction

1   Relevance of Designing for Interaction on Mobile Devices

> *"I felt that there was an opportunity to create a new design discipline,*
> *dedicated to creating imaginative and attractive solutions in a virtual world,*
> *where one could design behaviors, animations, and sounds as well as shapes.*
> *This would be the equivalent of industrial design*
> *but in software rather than three-dimensional objects."*
>
> -   *Bill Moggridge (2007, p. 14)*

In the above statement, Bill Moggridge, who designed the first laptop computer and founded the influential design firm IDEO, laid out the foundation for a new profession named *Interaction Design*, which is at the core of this dissertation. Our research is rooted in the observation that digital technology has fundamentally changed the way humans interact with objects. As a consequence, the focus of product development and design processes has been shifting away from creating physical objects towards designing for interaction with digital objects. Touch-based mobile devices play an essential role in this shift of design paradigms: "The cell phone is an example of the convergence of digital and physical interaction; in one product the design for sight, sound, and touch are all crucial" (Moggridge, 2007).

Over the past decade, mobile devices such as smartphones and tablet PCs have been steadily growing in economic importance. In the U.S. alone, mobile commerce accounted for more than 20 percent of online sales at the end of 2016 and will grow to almost 50 percent by 2020 (Statista, 2017). Advertising spending on mobile devices is predicted to total more than $58 billion in 2017 (eMarketer, 2017). Mobile currently represents roughly 70 percent of digital ad investment, with its share forecasted to be growing to close to 80 percent by 2021. This trend is fueled by the rapid spread and adoption of smartphones and tablets around the world. Globally, the number of smartphone users reached 2.1 billion in 2016, and is expected to rise to 2.87 billion in 2020 (Statista, 2016a). The number of tablet users worldwide is growing at a similar pace, from 1.12 billion in 2016 to 1.46 billion in 2020 (Statista, 2016b). Correspondingly, mobile devices play an increasingly important role in private and social life. More and more time is spent with smartphones, tablets, and hybrid "phablets" (Flurry Analytics, 2016).

This dissertation builds on two main characteristics of mobile devices. First, most devices nowadays are equipped with touchscreens (DeviceAtlas, 2016) that provide the opportunity to design for multisensory digital product experiences. Second, in contrast to traditional desktop PCs, smartphones and tablets are truly personal and highly individualized devices (Bacile et al., 2014). Through the combination of these properties, touch interfaces – in particular when personally owned – can reduce media discontinuity and allow consumers to exercise more direct control when evaluating products online (Hein et al., 2011; Brasel and Gips, 2014; 2015).

2   Contribution of the Dissertation

The topic of designing for interaction on mobile devices has attracted interest from researchers of various disciplines. This dissertation is primarily rooted in the fields of management, marketing, information systems, and psychology – however, we also frequently relate to human-computer interaction research which puts more emphasis on the development and evaluation of new technologies that facilitate the digital touch experience. As further discussed in the following articles, the haptic information framework proposed by Peck and Childers (2003b) provides a meaningful way to segment existing literature. Within our scope of mobile interaction design, we distinguish between product-, interface-, and consumer-related factors. Product-related factors such as object properties, touchability and intangibility have been mainly discussed in management and marketing research (e.g. Peck and Childers, 2003a; Peck and Wiggins, 2006; Peck and Shu, 2009; Kim and Krishnan, 2015). Interface-related factors comprise both a hardware side (i.e., the device and digital screen as a medium) and a software side (i.e., the digital representation of an object in the virtual world). While early research on virtual product experiences was focused on traditional web interfaces (e.g., Schlosser, 2003; Grohmann et al., 2007), an increasing number of studies have investigated the specific capabilities of touch-based mobile interfaces in recent years (e.g., Brasel and Gips, 2014; Brasel and Gips, 2015; Shen et al., 2016). With regard to digital interaction, Jiang and Benbasat (2005) distinguish between visual control mechanisms (i.e., technologies enabling customizable presentation formats and navigation) and functional control mechanisms (i.e., technologies enabling virtual exploration of product-specific features and functions). Such interactive technologies are particularly discussed in information systems (e.g., Jiang and Benbasat, 2007; De et al., 2013) and psychology (e.g., Overmars and Poels, 2015; Blazquez Cano et al., 2017). Lastly, consumer-related factors such as need for touch, goal orientation, perceived diagnosticity or perceived ownership are broadly discussed in all disciplines, particularly marketing (e.g., Peck and Childers, 2003a; Schlosser et al., 2006; Elder and Krishna, 2012).

Our corresponding research objectives are as follows. First, we provide a holistic overview of research from multiple disciplines on the topic of exploring products through digital touch. As outlined above, our goal is to distill product-, interface-, and consumer-related factors to be considered when designing for interaction on mobile devices. This segmentation lays the foundation for the three subsequent research questions addressed in this dissertation. Second, we focus on the product perspective and aim to develop a tool that helps organizations to quantify, visualize, and communicate the user experience of their digital products. Third, we focus on the digital touch interface per se. Our objective is to gain an understanding of how digital interaction design, particularly through visual control mechanisms, might entail different effects on touch-based mobile devices relative to traditional desktop PCs. Lastly, we focus on a consumer point of view and investigate how goal orientation influences the relationship between different mobile user interfaces, consumer attitudes, and behavioral intentions. The resulting structure of this dissertation is detailed in the following section.

3   Structure of the Dissertation and Summary of Articles

This cumulative dissertation is structured as follows. After this introduction, we present four different articles. The first article provides a systematic literature review of articles that discuss the exploration of products through digital touch. We analyze and synthesize research from different disciplines to build the theoretical foundation for the remaining articles, clustered into the focal areas of the product, the interface, and the individual consumer. The second article is product-focused: we bridge the gap between academia and practice by proposing a formalism and corresponding tool to quantify, visualize, and communicate a product's user experience within organizations. The third article focuses on the digital touch interface, and deals with the effects of visual control mechanisms on touch-based mobile devices as well as the role of textural fit between the surfaces of products and touchscreens. In the fourth article, which focuses on the individual consumer, we investigate the effects of goal-oriented mobile user interfaces on cognitive and affective reactions as well consumer attitudes. At the end, we provide an overall conclusion that consists of a concise summary and outlines managerial implications as well as opportunities for future research.

The overall structure of this dissertation is visualized in Figure 1.

Figure 1. Structure of the dissertation.

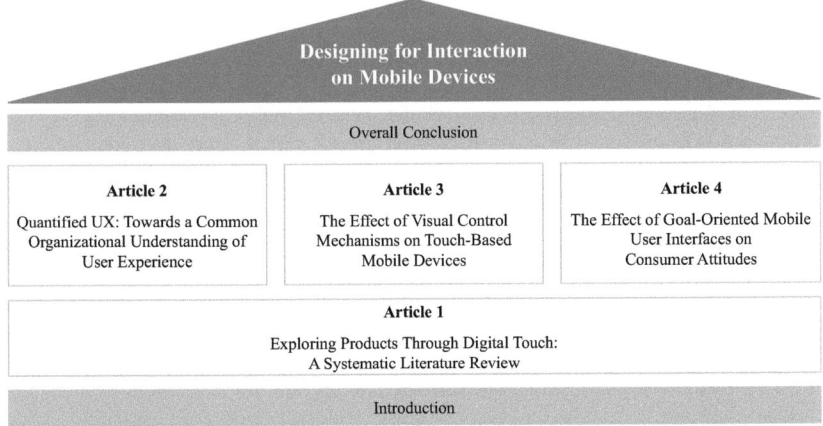

Data. Article 1 provides a systematic literature review of 31 articles published in 13 different journals in the fields of management, marketing, information systems, and psychology. We develop an analytical framework and categorize our findings into 15 different product-, interface-, and consumer-related factors influencing the digital touch experience. In Article 2, we develop a tool to quantify, visualize, and communicate user experience. Our work is based on 30 articles from six different conference proceedings and journals as well as 24 interviews with experts from academia and practice. Moreover, we evaluate our tool by integrating it into the product design processes of three different companies. The dataset in Article 3, which is used to analyze consumer choice on mobile devices, stems from an affiliate shopping website for lifestyle and fashion products, and one of their largest partner shops, a leading European online fashion retailer. It comprises 467,132 observations in 193,255 distinct user sessions. In addition, we collect survey data comprising 804 respondents on Amazon Mechanical Turk to investigate the role of textural fit on consumers' willingness to pay. Article 4 relies on survey data as well, with 399 subjects participating via Amazon Mechanical Turk. Here, our focus is to understand the impact of goal orientation on the relationship between different versions of mobile user interface design on consumers attitudes.

Methods. Throughout this dissertation, we make use of a variety of different methods to analyze the qualitative and quantitative data obtained. In Article 1, we follow the approach by Webster and Watson (2002) to structure our literature search. For the analysis part, we build upon the haptic information framework as proposed by Peck and Childers (2003b) to cluster our findings. Lastly, we develop a research agenda based on Mahajan and Venkatesh (2000) as well as Parasuraman and Zinkhan (2002). Our approach in Article 2 is once again a systematic literature search based on Webster and Watson (2002). In our subsequent analysis, we follow the grounded theory approach (Glaser and Strauss, 1971; Isabella, 1990). Finally, we use qualitative content analysis as proposed by Mayring (2014) for our expert interviews. Our field experiment in Article 3 contains two-stage panel data, which we model as binary choice equations that account for session-specific, product-specific, and time-specific variables. Our empirical analysis is based on a Heckman selection model (Heckman, 1979) as specified by Cameron and Trivedi (2010). We use an OLS regression model to analyze the corresponding online experiment. Article 4 focuses on a variety of moderating and mediating effects, which we illustrate through a path analysis (Preacher and Hayes, 2004; Hayes, 2013). Furthermore, we conduct several tests to compare our different treatment groups, both parametric (two-sample t-tests with equal variances) and non-parametric (Wilcoxon rank-sum tests, to account for smaller group sizes).

Table 1 provides a concise overview of the foci, objectives, data, methods, and key findings for each of the four articles.

Table 1. Foci, objectives, data, method, and key findings.

Article	Article 1 Exploring Products Through Digital Touch: A Systematic Literature Review	Article 2 Quantified UX: Towards a Common Organizational Understanding of User Experience	Article 3 The Effect of Visual Control Mechanisms on Touch-Based Mobile Devices	Article 4 The Effect of Goal-Oriented Mobile User Interfaces on Consumer Attitudes
Focus	Overview	Product	Interface	Consumer
Objective	Review of previous research in marketing, management, information systems and psychology literature	Development of a formalism and corresponding tool to measure, visualize, and communicate a product's UX within organizations	Analysis of consumer choice and willingness to pay when enabling visual control mechanisms on mobile devices	Analysis of consumers' goal orientation with respect to mobile user interface design
Data	Scientific articles published in 13 different academic journals N = 31 articles	Scientific articles published in six different conference proceedings and journals; expert interviews; evaluation N = 30 articles; N = 24 interviews N = 3 companies for tool evaluation	Field data from leading European fashion retailer; survey data from Amazon MTurk experiment N = 467,132 obs. in 193,255 sessions; N = 804 survey participants	Survey data from Amazon MTurk experiment N = 399 survey participants
Method	Systematic literature review	Grounded theory; qualitative content analysis	Heckman selection model; OLS	Path analysis; parametric and nonparametric tests
Key Findings	Experiencing products through digital touch is driven by product-, interface-, and consumer-related factors; the topic has been primarily discussed in marketing literature; future research should focus more on observational data	Quantifying and visualizing a product's UX helps organizations prioritize, allows for benchmarking, and facilitates communication in teams	The effect of alternative photo technology on consumer choice is negative on PCs but positive on mobile devices; textural fit between product and touchscreen moderates the digital touch experience	Goal orientation mediates consumer perceptions and attitudes; consumer attitudes toward certain mobile UI design combinations differ depending on goal orientation

Article 1.
Exploring Products Through Digital Touch: A Systematic Literature Review

Our first article lays the foundation of this dissertation and addresses the challenge of how to compensate for haptic product experiences in light of an increasing number of consumers shopping online via computer-mediated interfaces. In a systematic literature review, we explore and discuss the corresponding contextual factors and underlying psychological mechanisms. Adapting a multidisciplinary point of view, we identify, structure, and analyze relevant studies from the fields of management, marketing, information systems and psychology. Starting from a total of 222 articles which meet our initial search criteria, we narrow down our sample to 31 articles published in 13 different journals. Then, we distill our findings and develop an analytical framework that distinguishes between product-, interface-, and consumer-related factors influencing the digital touch experience. In the final step, we provide a comprehensive agenda that outlines some of the main theory-, data-, method- and technology-related challenges to be addressed in future research.

Article 2.
Quantified UX: Towards a Common Organizational Understanding of User Experience

The second article of this dissertation is motivated by the frequent misunderstandings and inefficiencies in industrial practice when it comes to the user experience (UX) of digital products. While UX is increasingly being recognized as an essential factor for commercial success, it has recently become a buzzword that lacks a commonly shared understanding, let alone definition. Against this background, therefore, we propose a quantifiable way of describing User Experience (QUX). Our analysis is based on 84 existing UX evaluation methods, a sample of UX characteristics derived from 30 different articles published in relevant conference proceedings, and 24 interviews with experts from academia and practice. As a result, we develop a formalism and a corresponding tool to measure, visualize, and communicate a product's UX within organizations. The benefits of our approach are showcased through the integration of our tool into the product development processes of companies which operate in three different industries: QUX helps organizations to prioritize, it allows for benchmarking with competitors as well as over time, and it facilitates communication in teams. Overall, we see QUX as complementary to the landscape of existing UX evaluation methods and as a solid foundation for future work towards a common organizational understanding of UX.

Article 3.
The Effect of Visual Control Mechanisms on Touch-Based Mobile Devices

The focus of our third article is to investigate the interaction effects between digital touchscreen interfaces and visual control mechanisms on consumer choice and willingness to pay. In two experimental studies, we examine the effects of the most frequently used visual control mechanisms, *zoom technology* and *alternative photo technology*. First, we provide empirical data from a field experiment comprising of 467,132 observations in 193,255 unique sessions along two stages of the buying process, product interest and product purchase. We are particularly interested in the moderating role of touchscreen interfaces. Therefore, we single out customers who used touch-based mobile devices such as smartphones and tablets, and explore interaction effects with zoom and alternative photo technology. Second, we conduct an online experiment on mobile devices with 804 subjects to gain further insights into how the relationship between visual control mechanisms and consumers' willingness to pay is influenced by the degree of textural fit between a touchscreen and the surfaces of different products. Findings from both experiments indicate that alternative photo technology leads to decreased product interest but higher willingness to pay, whereas zoom technology seems to have no comparable effects. Furthermore, we demonstrate that these effects of visual control mechanisms differ in both magnitude and direction between touch-based mobile devices and non-touch PC interfaces. Lastly, textural fit is established as an essential driver of object valuation on touch devices. In conclusion, our study reveals stark contrasts between different types of visual control and contributes to the understanding of their interplay with product-specific characteristics as well as consumer touch points across device types.

Article 4.
The Effect of Goal-Oriented Mobile User Interfaces on Consumer Attitudes

The fourth and final article of this dissertation deals with the observation that smartphones are increasingly used for various types of product research, which fall into the broad categories of either casual browsing or target search. Since modern mobile web design is responsive to device-related restrictions such as screen size but does not consider consumer-related characteristics such as goal orientation, our online experiment, which comprises 399 participants, investigates the moderating effect of consumer goals on the relationship between consumer perceptions of and attitudes. Our results indicate that browsers are primarily influenced by enjoyment, while searchers tend to care more about diagnosticity. Furthermore, we address the question of how goal-oriented mobile user interface (UI) design affects consumer attitudes towards shopping at the website. We manipulate three factors in our online experiment: *interaction technique* (vertical scrolling vs. horizontal swiping), *screen layout* (one vs. three products displayed simultaneously), and *assortment size* (six vs. 15 products to choose from). The resulting eight different treatment groups are analyzed through parametric and nonparametric tests and show that consumer attitudes toward different combinations of UI design elements differ substantially depending on goal orientation. In summary, our findings suggest that goal orientation of individual consumers should play a more prominent role in mobile user interface design considerations.

References

Bacile, T. J., Ye, C., & Swilley, E. (2014). From firm-controlled to consumer-contributed: Consumer co-production of personal media marketing communication. *Journal of Interactive Marketing, 28*(2), 117–133.

Blazquez Cano, M., Perry, P., Ashman, R., & Waite, K. (2017). The influence of image interactivity upon user engagement when using mobile touch screens. *Computers in Human Behavior*, 1–7.

Brasel, S. A., & Gips, J. (2014). Tablets, touchscreens, and touchpads: How varying touch interfaces trigger psychological ownership and endowment. *Journal of Consumer Psychology, 24*(2), 226–233.

Brasel, S. A., & Gips, J. (2015). Interface Psychology: Touchscreens Change Attribute Importance, Decision Criteria, and Behavior in Online Choice. *Cyberpsychology, Behavior, and Social Networking, 18*(9), 534–538.

Cameron, A. C., & Trivedi, P. K. (2010). *Microeconometrics using Stata*. Stata Press.

De, P., Hu, Y. (Jeffrey), & Rahman, M. S. (2013). Product-Oriented Web Technologies and Product Returns: An Exploratory Study. *Information Systems Research, 24*(4), 998–1010.

DeviceAtlas. (2016). Most popular viewport size statistics for 2016. Retrieved September 16, 2017, from https://deviceatlas.com/blog/viewport-size-statistics-2016.

Elder, R. S., & Krishna, A. (2012). The "Visual Depiction Effect" in Advertising: Facilitating Embodied Mental Simulation through Product Orientation. *Journal of Consumer Research, 38*(6), 988–1003.

eMarketer. (2017). US Ad Spending: eMarketer's Updated Estimates and Forecast for 2017. Retrieved September 20, 2017, from https://www.emarketer.com/Report/US-Ad-Spending-eMarketers-Updated-Estimates-Forecast-2017/2002134.

Flurry Analytics. (2016). Media, Productivity & Emojis Give Mobile Another Stunning Growth Year. Retrieved September 20, 2017, from http://flurrymobile.tumblr.com/post/136677391508/stateofmobile2015?soc_src=mail&soc_trk=ma.

Glaser, B. G., & Strauss, A. L. (1971). *The Discovery of Grounded Theory: Strategies for Qualitative Research. American Sociological Review* (Vol. 36). New Jersey: Aldine Transaction.

Grohmann, B., Spangenberg, E. R., & Sprott, D. E. (2007). The influence of tactile input on the evaluation of retail product offerings. *Journal of Retailing, 83*(2), 237–245.

Hayes, A. F. (2013). *Introduction to mediation, moderation, and conditional process analysis*. Guilford Press.

Heckman, J. J. (1979). Sample Selection Bias as a Specification Error. *Econometrica, 47*(1), 153.

Isabella, L. A. (1990). Evolving Interpretations as a Change Unfolds: How Managers Construe Key Organizational Events. *Academy of Management Journal, 33*(1), 7–41.

Jiang, Z., & Benbasat, I. (2005). Virtual Product Experience: Effects of Visual and Functional Control of Products on Perceived Diagnosticity and Flow in Electronic Shopping. *Journal of Management Information Systems, 21*(3), 111–147.

Jiang, Z., & Benbasat, I. (2007). Investigating the influence of the functional mechanisms of online product presentations. *Information Systems Research, 18*(4), 454–470.

Kim, Y., & Krishnan, R. (2015). On Product-Level Uncertainty and Online Purchase Behavior: An Empirical Analysis. *Management Science, 61*(10), 2449–2467.

Mahajan, V., & Venkatesh, R. (2000). Marketing modeling for e-business. *International Journal of Research in Marketing, 17*(2–3), 215–225.

Mayring, P. (2014). *Qualitative Content Analysis Theoretical Foundation, Basic Procedures and Software Solution.* Retrieved from http://www.ssoar.info/ssoar/bitstream/handle/document/39517/ssoar-2014-mayring-Qualitative_content_analysis_theoretical_foundation.pdf.

Moggridge, B. (2007). *Designing interactions.* MIT Press. Retrieved from https://mitpress.mit.edu/books/designing-interactions.

Overmars, S., & Poels, K. (2015). Online product experiences: The effect of simulating stroking gestures on product understanding and the critical role of user control. *Computers in Human Behavior, 51*(PA), 272–284.

Parasuraman, A., & Zinkhan, G. M. (2002). Marketing to and Serving Customers through the Internet: An Overview and Research Agenda. *Journal of the Academy of Marketing Science, 30*(4), 286–295.

Peck, J., & Childers, T. L. (2003a). Individual Differences in Haptic Information Processing: The "Need for Touch" Scale. *Journal of Consumer Research, 30*(3), 430–442.

Peck, J., & Childers, T. L. (2003b). To Have and To Hold: The Influence of Haptic Information on Product Judgments. *Journal of Marketing, 67*(2), 35–48.

Peck, J., & Shu, S. B. (2009). The Effect of Mere Touch on Perceived Ownership. *Journal of Consumer Research, 36*(3), 434–447.

Peck, J., & Wiggins, J. (2006). It Just Feels Good: Customers' Affective Response to Touch and Its Influence on Persuasion. *Journal of Marketing, 70*(4), 56–69.

Preacher, K. J., & Hayes, A. F. (2004). SPSS and SAS procedures for estimating indirect effects in simple mediation models. *Behavior Research Methods, Instruments, & Computers, 36*(4), 717–731.

Schlosser, A. E. (2003). Experiencing Products in the Virtual World: The Role of Goal and Imagery in Influencing Attitudes versus Purchase Intentions. *Journal of Consumer Research, 30*(2), 184–198.

Schlosser, A. E., White, T. B., & Lloyd, S. M. (2006). Converting Web Site Visitors into Buyers: How Web Site Investment Increases Consumer Trusting Beliefs and Online Purchase Intentions. *Journal of Marketing, 70*(2), 133–148.

Shen, H., Zhang, M., & Krishna, A. (2016). Computer Interfaces and the "Direct-Touch" Effect: Can iPads Increase the Choice of Hedonic Food? *Journal of Marketing Research, 53*(5), 745–758.

Statista. (2016a). Number of smartphone users worldwide 2014-2020. Retrieved September 20, 2017, from https://www.statista.com/statistics/330695/number-of-smartphone-users-worldwide/.

Statista. (2016b). Tablet users worldwide 2013-2020. Retrieved September 20, 2017, from https://www.statista.com/statistics/377977/tablet-users-worldwide-forecast/.

Statista. (2017). Mobile commerce in the United States - Statistics & Facts. Retrieved September 13, 2017, from https://www.statista.com/topics/1185/mobile-commerce/.

Webster, J., & Watson, R. T. (2002). Analyzing the past to prepare for the future: Writing a literature review. *MIS Quarterly*, *26*(2), xiii–xxiii.

II   Article 1

Exploring Products Through Digital Touch:
A Systematic Literature Review[1]

Abstract

Nowadays, more and more people shop for products online. This phenomenon presents researchers and practitioners alike with the challenge of how to compensate for haptic product experiences on computer-mediated interfaces. Over the past decade, however, the rapid adoption of mobile touch devices such as smartphones and tablets created new opportunities to provide multisensory virtual product experiences. Our work addresses the following research question: what are the contextual factors and psychological mechanisms driving the digital touch experience? We present a systematic approach to identify, structure, and analyze relevant studies from the disciplines of management, marketing, information systems and psychology. Starting from a total of 142 journals meeting our selection criteria, we narrow down our sample to 31 articles published in 13 different journals. To provide an overview, we map out and discuss product-, interface-, and consumer-related factors influencing the digital touch experience. Lastly, we develop a comprehensive agenda for future research that outlines some of the main theory-, data-, method- and technology-related challenges to be addressed in the coming years.

Keywords: *touch, haptics, computer interfaces, mobile, online shopping, literature review*

---

[1] This article is based on the following working paper: Naegelein, P. (2017). *Exploring Products Through Digital Touch: A Systematic Literature Review*. Working Paper. LMU Munich.

1   Introduction

*"Estimates are that it will be fifteen years
before a good replication of touch is perfected."*

CNN Moneyline, 2000

The above statement is cited in Peck and Childers' seminal work on the role of haptic information and consumers' individual need for touch when judging products (2003a, 2003b). In the early 2000s, with online shopping and non-touch media on the rise, scholars began to research how to compensate for actual, physical touch of products in computer-mediated interfaces. About fifteen years later, touch-based mobile devices such as tablets and smartphones have been widely adopted, with mobile commerce and ad spending growing rapidly (Bart et al., 2014; Grewal et al., 2016). While it could be argued to what degree a good replication of touch has become possible, a small but growing literature field is analyzing product experience through digital touch.

The general research question guiding this work is the following: What are the contextual factors and psychological mechanisms driving the digital touch experience? So far, we know of no comprehensive and structured analysis addressing the above research question. To address these issues, the objective of this study is to provide a systematic literature review of previous research on touch modalities and mobile shopping – a topic area of interest to multiple disciplines. Hence, we follow a systematic approach as suggested by Webster and Watson (2002), considering peer-reviewed articles published in the disciplines of management, marketing, information systems, and psychology.

Our analytical framework is derived from Peck and Childers (2003b) and distinguishes between product-, interface-, and consumer-related factors influencing digital touch. Specifically, we investigate how these factors influence each other and consumer decisions overall. While management and marketing literature broadly discuss all of three angles, information systems and psychology literature mostly focus on interface- and consumer-related questions.

The remainder of this work is structured as follows. Section 2 introduces our methodological approach, covering our data collection process, analytical framework, and data analysis. Section 3 is divided into two parts. First, we describe the identified literature to structure and map our findings. Second, we analyze the results of the systematic literature review, explaining and analyzing the product-, interface-, and consumer-related factors we identified. A research agenda clustered into theory-, data-, method-, and technology-related challenges follows in Section 4. Section 5 concludes.

2   Methodology

To answer our research question, we conducted a systematic literature review as defined by Jesson et al. (2011) and follow the methodology proposed by Webster and Watson (2002). In this section, we outline our data collection process, analytical framework, and analysis.

2.1   Data Collection

To start with, we defined relevant disciplines: marketing, psychology, information systems, and management. The topic area of digital touch combines a variety of literature streams. In our context, *marketing* literature discusses the role of product touch in different retail settings. The underlying mechanisms are subject to many studies in consumer *psychology*. Literature on *information systems* frequently discusses technology-enabled digital touch mechanisms, and lastly, *management* literature focuses on the business rather than the consumer perspective. We did not include human computer-interaction literature, since its focus on technological advancements and usability studies is beyond the scope of this review.

Next, we compiled a list of the most relevant peer-reviewed journals within the four disciplines. Therefore, we relied on VHB-JOURQUAL rating (third edition, published in 2015) which is frequently used to assess journal's reputation and quality in management research (Schrader and Hennig-Thurau, 2009). We focused on the subcategories "management", "marketing", and "information systems", considering all journals awarded with an "A+", "A", or "B" rating (see Appendix A.1). Since psychology literature is not covered in the VHB JOURQUAL rating, we used a different measure to identify relevant outlets in this field: the Journal Citation Report by Thomson Reuters (e.g., Lorenz and Löffler, 2015). It calculates a journal's impact factor, which is based on the average number of its articles' citations – thus, the impact factor should be considered a measure of relevance rather than quality. Within the social sciences edition, we considered all journals in the area of "multidisciplinary psychology" with an impact factor of 2 or higher (see Appendix A.2). In total, our full list comprises 142 journals, thereof 38 from management, 32 from marketing, 39 from information systems and 33 from psychology.

Then, we searched the SCOPUS database which includes all references and abstracts of the journals under consideration. Our search strategy comprised three steps, summarized in Table 1.

In the first step, we conducted an initial online search using the terms (mobile OR "virtual product experience") AND (touch OR haptic OR gesture). We defined rather broad search terms to account for the many different expressions that have come with technological advancements during the past two decades (e.g., mobile devices would include laptops, handhelds, mobile phones, smartphones, tablets, etc.). Using our journal list as a filter, we identified 222 publications.

Table 1. Relevant journals, their category, and number of articles considered based on three step selection process.

Academic Journal	Category	(1) Initial online search	(2) Excluded based on abstract	(3) Added by snow-balling	Final
Computers in Human Behavior	Psychology	100	-97	0	3
Frontiers in Psychology	Psychology	32	-32	0	0
Information Systems Research	IS	4	-4	+2	2
Journal of Advertising	Marketing	2	-1	+1	2
Journal of Business Research	Management	5	-4	+1	2
Journal of Consumer Psychology	Marketing	2	-1	+2	3
Journal of Consumer Research	Marketing	5	-4	+4	5
Journal of Interactive Marketing	Marketing	8	-6	+1	3
Journal of Management Information Systems	IS	3	-2	0	1
Journal of Marketing	Marketing	3	-3	+3	3
Journal of Marketing Research	Marketing	2	-1	0	1
Journal of Retailing	Marketing	5	-5	+3	3
Management Information Systems Quarterly	IS	0	0	+1	1
Management Science	Management	2	-2	+2	2
Other Academic Journals	Div.	49	-49	0	0
Total		222	-211	+20	31

In a second step, we scanned all abstracts and excluded articles which do not address our research question. As illustrated in Table 1, the number of publications within our initial sample that we found not be relevant (n = 211) to our research question was unusually high. This constellation can be largely attributed to the term "touch", which is used in many different settings. Most of our excluded articles were published in the field of psychology, and oftentimes focused on the role of touch and touch devices in children's learning environments. Within business research, for instance, a number of studies were not considered because they discuss touch points along the customer journey, unrelated to product haptics. Despite the low turnout, we chose to stick to our initial search terms in order to reliably capture the few highly relevant articles as a foundation for our subsequent analysis.

Thus, in our third step, we used a snowballing approach and scanned the references of our remaining 11 publications (both citing and cited). This way, we identified another 20 articles which matched the scope of our literature review. Finally, we ended up with a final number of 31 articles for our analysis.

2.2   Analytical Framework

We derive our analytical framework for this study from Peck and Childers (2003b). Their *Haptic Information Framework* describes three distinct but interrelated factors that affect the touch experience. First, product-related factors consider that physical products tend to differ substantially from one another with regard to their object properties (e.g., Klatzky and Lederman, 1993). Even though a substantial part of product information is gathered via senses other than touch, the haptic system seems to dominate all other senses during the decision-making process (Lederman and Klatzky, 1987). Second, situation-related factors describe the overall setting within which products are evaluated (Bloch and Richins, 1983). While traditional retailers such as brick-and-mortar stores might experiment with different in-store setups and presentation modes, an increasing part of shopping occurs via media such as catalogues, home-shopping television, or the internet. Third, consumer-related factors consider that individuals prefer different types of information (e.g., visual, verbal, or haptic; Childers et al., 1985) when forming purchasing decisions. Furthermore, they might show different cognitive and affective reactions when presented with the opportunity to experience a product through the sense of touch. Taken together, consumer preferences for online shopping formats are jointly driven by product-, situation-, and consumer-related characteristics which jointly influence the decision-making process (Alba et al., 1997; Citrin et al., 2003).

Our analytical framework is illustrated in Figure 1. Similar to Peck and Childers (2003b), we consider product- and consumer-related factors, adding new insights from business and psychology research. The main difference, however, is that we do not discuss situation-related factors per se, but focus on interface-related factors. More precisely, we discuss the role of digital interfaces such as smartphones and tablets, which mediate the touch experience and are thus at the core of this literature review. We deliberately do not cover situational factors such as time, location or context of mobile phone usage. While these considerations are closely related, they are beyond the scope of our research question.

Figure 1. Analytical framework (adapted from Peck and Childers, 2003b).

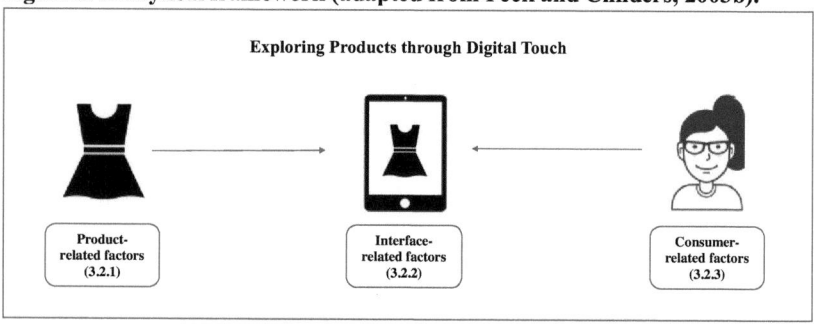

2.3   Data Analysis

We reviewed our selected papers using qualitative content analysis (Mayring, 2014). First, we followed the procedure of inductive category formation to distill all product-, interface-, and consumer-related factors mentioned in our final set of 31 articles. These categories were iteratively developed further during our research process and are described in the following section (3.1). Second, we created a classification matrix to provide an overview of which discipline and category our relevant factors can be attributed to (section 3.1). Lastly, we provide an in-depth discussion of all concepts which appeared twice or more (section 3.2).

3   Systematic Literature Review

The following section illustrates the descriptive results of our literature research and provides an in-depth analysis of the product-, interface-, and consumer-related factors identified.

3.1   Descriptive Results

Table 2 summarizes all journals our selected articles were published in. It becomes obvious that our research question is primarily addressed by marketing literature, with 20 relevant articles published in 7 different journals. This observation suggests that the topic of digital touch is, at its core, a question particularly relevant to marketing researchers since it builds upon prior work about product haptics and touch experience in traditional, brick-and mortar retail settings.

Table 2. Number of journals and articles by discipline.

Discipline	# Journals	Journal Names	# Articles
Management	2	Management Science, Journal of Business Research	**4**
Marketing	7	Journal of Advertising, Journal of Consumer Psychology, Journal of Consumer Research, Journal of Interactive Marketing, Journal of Marketing, Journal of Marketing Research, Journal of Retailing	**20**
Info. Systems	3	Information Systems Research, Journal of Management Information Systems,	**4**
Psychology	1	Computers in Human Behavior	**3**

As illustrated in figure 2, a clear trend suggesting increasing relevance of the topic is not yet visible. 2003 was the year when most studies were published (n=5) – ever since, no more than 3 relevant articles appeared per year. Note, however, that three out of four considered management studies and all three of the considered psychology studies were published in 2014 or later (cf. Table 5).

Figure 2. Number of relevant articles published per year.

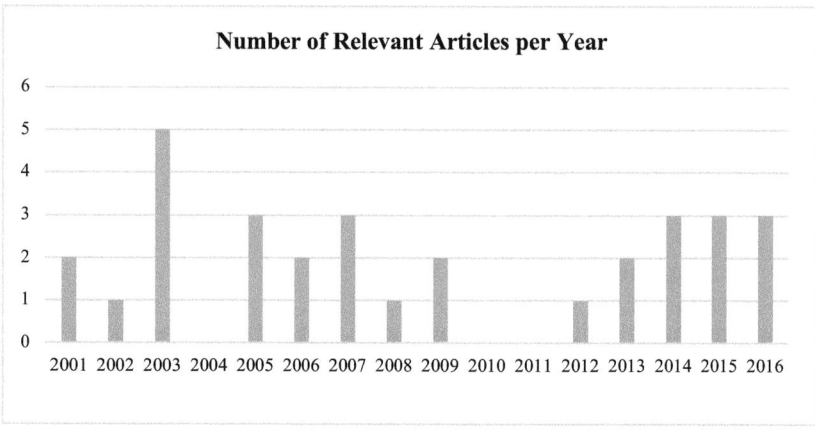

From our 31 articles, we were able to distill 15 factors influencing the digital touch experience which occurred in two or more articles. Product-related factors comprise product attributes as well as the concepts of intangibility, touchability, and touch valence. Interface-related factors are the degree of interface touch, visual control mechanisms, as well as object interactivity and vividness. As for consumer-related factors, we consider need for touch, goal orientation, perceived diagnosticity, affective reaction, mental simulation, perceived control, and perceived ownership. Table 3 provides an overview including brief explanations and number of occurrences, and section 3.2 analyzes these concepts in the respective order.

Table 3. Overview of factors influencing the digital touch experience.

	Factor	Explanation	Occurences
Product-related factors	Product Attributes	Classification of objects into different categories based on their specific properties.	4
	Intangibility	Degree to which product attributes are difficult to evaluate through the human senses.	5
	Touchability	Degree to which products encourage touch.	2
	Touch Valence	Type and strength of haptic sensory feedback.	2
Interface-related factors	Interface Touch	Degree to which computer-mediated interfaces allow for digital touch.	6
	Visual Control	Customizable presentation formats and navigation.	7
	Object Interactivity	Direct manipulation of virtual objects.	6
	Vividness	Involvement of multiple sensory channels through enriched multimedia.	7
Consumer-related factors	Need for Touch	Individual preference for haptic information.	7
	Goal Orientation	Consumer goals in online shopping (search vs browse).	2
	Perceived Diagnosticity	Perceived ability of websites to increase product understanding.	5
	Affective Reaction	Emotional response to touching an object.	6
	Mental Simulation	Reenactment of multisensory experiences when exposed to virtual objects.	3
	Perceived Control	Degree to which consumers feel they can modify the shopping environment.	3
	Perceived Ownership	Feeling of being psychologically attached to an object.	3

In Table 4, we illustrate how many different product-, interface- and consumer-related factors are discussed across our four different disciplines. Please note that most articles deal with more than one factor, exploring mutual relationships between the associated variables.

Table 4. Number of occurrences by factor and discipline.

Factor x Discipline	Management	Marketing	Information Systems	Psychology	*Total*
Product-related factors	2	11	0	0	*13*
Interface-related factors	3	15	6	3	*27*
Consumer-related factors	2	19	5	3	*29*
Total	*8*	*45*	*11*	*6*	*/*

It stands out that all three factor categories are, above all, discussed in marketing literature (total n=45) – which is not surprising given the high number of related studies in our sample. Most interestingly, our articles from psychology and information systems focus solely on interface- and consumer-related characteristics, and do not dive into product characteristics at all. The few studies focusing on product-related factors stem from management and marketing literature. Overall, interface- and consumer-related factors are of similarly high interest across all disciplines. In Table 5, we provide a detailed classification matrix which clusters all 31 studies by factor and discipline.

Table 5. Classification matrix by factor and discipline.

Factor	Management Literature	Marketing Literature	Info. Systems Literature	Psychology Literature
		Product-Related Factors		
Product Attributes	Citrin et al. (2003)	Childers et al. (2001); McCabe and Nowlis (2003); Roggeveen et al. (2015)		
Intangibility	Kim and Krishnan (2015)	Peck and Childers, (2003a); Laroche et al. (2005); Peck and Wiggins (2006); Grohmann et al. (2007)		
Touchability		Schlosser (2003); Brasel and Gips (2014)		
Touch Valence		Peck and Wiggins (2006); Peck and Shu (2009)		
		Interface-Related Factors		
Interface Touch		Schlosser (2003); Grohmann et al. (2007); Peck and Shu (2009); Peck et al. (2013); Brasel and Gips (2014); Shen et al. (2016)		
Visual Control		Li et al. (2002); Fiore et al. (2005)	Jiang and Benbasat (2005); De et al. (2013)	Verhagen et al. (2014); Overmars and Poels (2015); Blazquez Cano et al. (2016)
Object Interactivity		Schlosser (2003); Fiore et al. (2005); Schlosser (2006)	Jiang and Benbasat (2007a); Jiang and Benbasat (2007b); De et al. (2013)	

Factor	Management Literature	Marketing Literature	Info. Systems Literature	Psychology Literature
Vividness	Choi and Taylor (2014); Kim and Krishnan (2015)	Coyle and Thorson (2001); Jin (2009); Peck et al. (2013); Roggeveen et al. (2015)	Jiang and Ben-basat (2007a)	
Consumer-Related Factors				
Need for Touch	Citrin et al. (2003); Choi and Taylor (2014)	Peck and Childers, (2003a); Peck and Childers (2003b); Peck and Wiggins (2006); Grohmann, et al. (2007); Brasel and Gips (2014)		
Goal Orientation		Schlosser (2003); Schlosser (2006)		
Perceived Diagnosticity		Li et al. (2002)	Jiang and Ben-basat (2005); Jiang and Ben-basat (2007a); Jiang and Ben-basat (2007b)	Overmars and Poels (2015)
Affective Reaction		Schlosser (2003); Peck and Wiggins (2006); Kim and Forsythe (2008); Jin (2009)	Jiang and Ben-basat (2007a)	Verhagen et al. (2014)
Mental Simulation		Schlosser (2003); Elder and Krishna (2012); Shen et al. (2016)		
Perceived Control		Peck and Shu (2013)	Jiang and Ben-basat (2005)	Overmars and Poels (2015)
Perceived Ownership		Peck and Shu (2009); Peck et al. (2013); Brasel and Gips (2014)		

3.2   Main Results

In the following subsections, we analyze the product-, interface-, and consumer-related factors influencing the digital touch experience. For each factor, we provide a brief explanation and discuss its role in management, marketing, information systems, and/or psychology literature.

3.2.1   Product-Related Factors

First, we start with an overview of product attributes which allow for the classification of objects into different categories. Then, we discuss different concepts related to product touch.

3.2.1.1   Product Attributes

Throughout consumer research literature, products and their attributes have been classified in many ways. One of the most commons methods is to categorize objects into *search, experience, and credence goods*. While the quality of search goods (such as a map, a chair, or a painting) can be assessed before purchase, experience goods (such as a musical performance or a bottle of wine) can only be evaluated during or after use, and credence goods (also referred to as post-experience goods, such as legal or insurance services) may never be verified at all (Nelson, 1970; 1974).

Another frequent distinction is made between *geometric and material properties* (Klatzky et al., 1993; Lederman and Klatzky, 1990). Both are search attributes, but they differ in an important way: while geometric attributes (such as the size or shape of a can of soda) rely on the modality of vision, the quality assessment of material attributes (such as texture, weight, or hardness of a piece of clothing) relies primarily on touch. Thus, material objects tend to be frequently purchased in offline, brick-and-mortar store environments where consumers are given the opportunity to evaluate products through the use of haptics (McCabe and Nowlis, 2003; Citrin et al., 2003).

In light of increased online shopping, Lal and Sarvary (1999) distinguish between *digital and non-digital attributes*. Within this dichotomy, nondigital attributes refer to the need of physically examining the actual product, e.g., to feel the material properties of a fashion item. Digital attributes, in contrast, can be communicated at low cost via the Internet – e.g., by providing product information such as written description or pictures, or offering reading samples when selling books online. The concept of distinguishing between *sensory and nonsensory attributes* (Degeratu et al., 2000) is closely related. Within this context, sensory attributes can be evaluated only through the (combined) use of the human senses, whereas nonsensory attributes can easily be communicated in written or verbal form. Again, all of the above fall into the category of search attributes as all relevant properties can be evaluated prior to a purchase decision.

Lastly, products can be characterized as *hedonic or utilitarian* (e.g., Dhar and Wertenbroch, 2000). This concept is closely linked to shopping motivations and goal orientation (Childers et al., 2001). Utilitarian items (such as office supply) correspond to cognition-driven, information-based product use, whereas hedonic goods (such as jewelry) relate to affect-driven, enjoyment-based consumption. Roggeveen et al. (2015) find that dynamic (compared to static) presentation formats facilitate the choice of hedonically superior alternatives for both search and experience goods.

3.2.1.2   Product Touch

Intangibility. Intangibility can be defined as "what cannot be seen, tasted, felt, heard, or smelled" (Kotler and Bloom, 1984) and has evolved into a multidimensional construct over the years (Laroche et al., 2001; 2005). The first component, *physical intangibility*, refers to the degree a product is inaccessible to any sensory experiences. Prominent examples include professional advice (e.g., from lawyers or doctors) and are frequently discussed in service marketing literature (e.g., McDougall and Snetsinger, 1990). Second, *generality* focuses on individual consumers and their difficulties to provide a precise definition or description of a certain product. Consider purchasing a smartphone: in such cases, most people are able to cite general product attributes (such as name, color, key features) but are oftentimes unable to tell about technical device specifications that differentiate one phone type from another (such as processing unit or storage technology). The third dimension, *mental intangibility*, refers to products that are hard to visualize in spite of physical tangibility – e.g., a car or aircraft engine are hard to grasp mentally for consumers lacking experience with and exposure to the respective inner workings and mechanics.

Overall, intangibility has been shown to have a strong effect on decision-making (Laroche et al., 2001), especially online when purchase decisions must be made without any prior physical product evaluations – even though this final step of direct touch has substantial impact (Peck and Childers, 2003a; Peck and Wiggins, 2006). Generally, customers tend to prefer retailers who allow them to touch their products before purchase, in particular when tactile input is important for quality assessment, e.g., for fashion items or consumer electronics (McCabe and Nowlis, 2003). Grohmann et al. (2007) show that the evaluation of material products is positively affected through tactile input which is diagnostic and when product quality is high.

But what is the effect of shopping on the Internet? Laroche et al. (2005) compare traditional brick-and-mortar stores with online shopping and demonstrate the consequences of intangibility on evaluation difficulty and perceived risk, since the lack of experiential product information creates uncertainty among consumers about subjective quality (Dimoka et al., 2012). As a consequence, product classifications can differ between the offline and online world. Kim and Krishnan (2015) use the example of a dress, which falls in the category of search goods in brick-and-mortar stores, but becomes and experience good in the online world where the opportunity of physical touch and try-on is not available. Hence, an intangibility level construct is developed to measure the lost information when shopping online, grasping consumers' difficulties in assessing the congruence between a product's attributes and their personal needs. Their real-word transaction data suggest a learning curve in evaluating subjective quality of intangible products: more and more purchases are made despite uncertainty when consumers' online shopping experience increases.

Touchability. Touchability is described as "the inherent tendency of the product to invite touch, particularly for hedonic purposes" (Klatzky and Peck, 2012; p. 140) and builds upon the conceptualization of a *visual preview model* (Klatzky et al., 1993). Consumers have a look at the respective product first and extract visual information, which is already sufficient for decision-making in many cases. For products who are rather material than geometric, however, touch is needed as a complementary source of information to assess use-related features such as weight or surface texture. In addition, attractive product design and smooth surfaces trigger hedonic touch, while rough surface textures and increasing shape complexity were shown to be less inviting to touch and feel (Klatzky and Peck, 2012). In addition, Schlosser (2003) found that the perceived touchability of products high in haptic importance increase mental simulation and, in turn, psychological ownership. Most recently, Brasel and Gips (2014) transferred this logic to shopping on touch-based mobile devices and showed that touchability moderates the relationship of digital touch and ownership feelings.

Touch valence. The concept of touch valence goes one step beyond touchability and refers to the sensory feedback when actually touching the product. Peck and Wiggins (2006) illustrate that touch elements providing positive sensory feedback (e.g., a feather) tend to increase persuasiveness of marketing messages, especially for consumers characterized by a high need for touch. In contrast, negative touch valence (e.g., when touching sand paper) can have a depressing effect on consumer attitudes. Furthermore, Peck and Shu (2009) examine the relationship between touch valence and object valuation. Their findings indicate that when product touch provides neutral or pleasant haptic sensory feedback, object valuation will increase through higher levels of affective reaction and perceived ownership. Conversely, unpleasant touch sensations could induce negative effects and thereby decrease object valuation as well endowment.

3.2.2   Interface-Related Factors

In our context of digital touch, interface-related factors comprise both a hardware component (i.e., the device and digital screen as a medium) and a software component (i.e., the digital representation of an object in the virtual world). Within this subsection, we first investigate the hardware side, focusing on the role of different device types characterized by varying degrees of interface touch. Then, following the conceptualization of virtual control proposed by Jiang and Benbasat (2005), we continue with the software side, distinguishing between visual control mechanisms (which describe technologies enabling customizable presentation formats and navigation) and functional control mechanisms (which allow for virtual exploration of product-specific features and functions).

3.2.2.1   Varying Degrees of Interface Touch

To date, the literature stream about the effect of computer-mediated interfaces such as touchscreens on consumer behavior is still in its infancy (see, e.g., Shen et al., 2016; Peck et al., 2013). Related research has mainly been conducted in the fields of human-computer interaction and multichannel shopping. For instance, Xu et al. (2017) examine the capabilities of tablet computers relative to PCs and smartphones, concluding that the tablet channel mostly complements the smartphone channel, while it substitutes the PC channel. Information systems literature discusses differences in screen size, portability, and resulting user behavior (e.g., Ghose et al., 2013; Adipat et al., 2011).

Within the context of consumer behavior, focus has recently shifted to the capabilities of touchscreen interfaces, which most mobile devices bring along. In how far can experiencing objects through digital touch interfaces resemble physically touching the actual product? Schlosser (2003) shows that perceived touchability of haptic products stimulates mental simulation and increases ownership feelings, especially when haptic characteristics are diagnostic (Grohmann et al., 2007; Peck and Shu, 2009) demonstrate that merely touching an object is sufficient to create perceived ownership.

Such feelings of possession can be increased using direct touch interfaces (compared to using touchpads and computer mouse devices) since the nature of interaction resembles direct physical touch more closely (Brasel and Gips, 2014). This analogy is moderated by interface ownership, driven by perceived control and associations of touch devices as the consumer's extended self (Brasel and Gips, 2014; Rudmin and Berry, 1987; Hein et al., 2011). Shen et al. (2016) illustrate how touchscreen interfaces enhance mental product interaction, facilitating the choice of affect-laden products such as hedonic food.

3.2.2.2   Visual Control Mechanisms

User experiences with products can be mapped on a continuum from direct (e.g., holding a product in the hands) to indirect (e.g., reading an advertisement or written product description, Mooy and Robben, 2002). When shopping online, consumer interaction with the product is usually restrained to computer-mediated, indirect experiences. To address this challenge, retailers increasingly rely on innovative presentation formats to reduce frictions and enable virtual product inspection (Li et al., 2002; Jiang and Benbasat, 2005).

It is shown that visual control (implemented through interactive 3D movies of the product) results in increased levels of perceived diagnosticity and cognitive enjoyment (Jiang and Benbasat, 2005). Meanwhile, advancements in web technology enable a myriad of interactive presentation formats. De et al. (2013), for instance, investigate the effect of zoom usage and alternative photo usage in online stores. Their empirical study indicates that, driven by increased factual information, the provision of zoom technology leads to fewer product returns, whereas alternative photo usage shows the opposite effect, potentially due to more unrealistic pre-purchase expectations. More recently, 360-degree product spin and virtual mirror technology have emerged (e.g., Verhagen et al., 2014). At least to some extent, the provision of 360-degree product view enhances virtual product experience in a sense that interaction resembles unmediated, brick-and-mortar retail settings more closely compared to the use of text and static images. Virtual mirror formats are driven by augmented reality technology and allow users to see the integration of virtual objects in the real world through the device's camera. Prominent examples include glasses (through the virtual mirror, user can explore how different glasses would look like on their own faces) or furniture (users can visualize how, for example, a certain couch would fit into their living room). Such presentation formats result in increased levels of presence, which lead to higher purchase intentions through increased product tangibility and likeability (Verhagen et al., 2014).

Image interactivity technology (IIT), described as "Web site features that enable creation and manipulation of product or environment images to simulate (or surpass) actual experience with the product or environment" (Fiore et al., 2005; Fiore and Jin, 2003), is viewed as a specific contributor to interactivity. Some main functionalities include interactive navigation or the ability to directly manipulate product design, viewing angle or distance – all enhancing product information through non-textual, (audio-)visual cues (Fiore et al., 2005). Overmars and Poels (2015) introduce an interface using IIT to simulate stroking gestures and demonstrate that the ability to exercise direct control (as opposed to passively watching a product video) induces tactile sensations which increase product understanding. Moreover, IIT has been shown to have positive effects on consumer engagement by contributing to multisensory enjoyment and entertainment value of the browsing experience (Blazquez Cano et al., 2016).

3.2.2.3   Functional Control Mechanisms

In his seminal work defining virtual reality, Steuer (1992) establishes two axial dimensions of functional control, determining how humans experience objects through a computer-mediated interface. The first dimension, interactivity, is about interaction with the virtual product itself. The second dimension, vividness, deals with the way information is conveyed towards users.

Functional control through (object) interactivity. Interactivity can be defined as "the extent to which users can participate in modifying the form and content of a mediated environment in real time" (Steuer, 1992). Schlosser (2003) refines this terminology introducing the concept of *object interactivity*, which describes the direct manipulation of a virtual object itself. Such direct manipulations are enabled by continuously changing product images resulting from user interactions similar to respective physical behavior (Shneiderman, 1987). In this regard, the concept of object interactivity is limited to functional control and substantially differs from visual control mechanisms that stem from, e.g., interactive navigation features such as product zoom, embedded search engines, or hyperlinks (Schlosser, 2006; De et al., 2013; Lynch and Ariely, 2000). Object interactivity, in contrast, directly refers to specific product features.

Schlosser (2003) investigates the influence of object interactivity on individual information processing. It is shown that virtual interaction with the product results in vivid mental imagery and increased purchase intentions, regardless of user goals. These higher levels of behavioral intentions are not limited to the examined product itself: when provided with the opportunity to customize product-specific attributes online, consumers tend to form more positive global attitudes to the overall online store (Fiore et al., 2005). Within this context, Jiang and Benbasat, 2007a) establish product diagnosticity as a mediator which is driven by both interactivity and vividness.

Functional control through vividness. Vividness, in this context oftentimes also referred to as "media richness" (e.g., Klein, 2003; Jin, 2009), is "likely to attract and hold our attention and to excite the imagination to the extent that it is (a) emotionally interesting, (b) concrete and imagery provoking, and (c) proximate in a sensory, temporal, or spatial way" (Nisbett and Ross, 1980, p. 45). Essentially, the more vividly information is presented, the more senses and pathways get involved in judgment and decision-making processes, likely resulting in increased cognitive engagement and amplification of pre-held attitudes and believes (e.g., Jiang and Benbasat, 2007a; Nisbett and Ross, 1980). Therefore, vividness is widely viewed as one of the most dominant factors affecting visual imagery (Burns et al., 1993; Bone and Ellen, 1992). Moreover, vivid elements were shown to increase stickiness since relevant information is more likely primed and stored in memory (Sherman et al., 1990).

Coyle and Thorson (2001) apply the perspective of vividness to websites. Building upon the contributing effect of vividness to telepresence (Steuer, 1992), it is proposed and shown that increased levels of vividness in a website result in heightened levels of telepresence and behavioral intentions. Since vivid presentation formats involve multiple sensory channels, attract higher levels of attention from consumers, and stimulate information processing, perceived diagnosticity is enhanced by increased levels of vividness (Jiang and Benbasat, 2007a). Furthermore, the vividness of mental imagery is associated with increased levels of perceived physical control and feelings of possession (Peck et al., 2013). In a series of experiments, participants were asked to imagine touching different products. It was shown that imagining touch with one's eyes closed comes remarkably close to touching the actual product: more vivid haptic imagery reinforces perceptions of control and ownership. Haptic imagery, thus, can serve as a surrogate for touch. Overall, the vividness of mental imagery can be considered a main driver of behavioral intentions in virtual environments (Choi and Taylor, 2014). In an empirical study, Kim and Krishnan (2015) investigate in how far more vivid (and interactive) video formats, compared to text and images, could enhance consumers' product understanding and their ability to evaluate quality and performance. They find that, among other, the use of digitized video commercials can serve to effectively reduce product-level uncertainty. Similarly, Roggeveen et al. (2015) show that dynamic presentation formats such as product videos increase consumer preference for hedonic products and their respective willingness to pay.

3.2.3   Consumer-Related Factors
Consumer-related factors affecting the digital touch experience can be either pre-existing (i.e., individual consumer characteristics) or induced via marketing stimuli (i.e., individual consumer perceptions and reactions).

3.2.3.1   Individual Characteristics
Need for touch. Consumers differ among one another in their individual preference for haptic information (Peck and Childers, 2003a). Particularly those who prefer product evaluation through direct touch express increasing levels of frustration when deprived of the opportunity to hold a product in their hands (Peck and Childers, 2003b). To account for such intra-individual differences, several scales were developed – most notably, need for tactile input (NTI; Citrin et al., 2003) and need for touch (NFT; Peck and Childers, 2003a). While the NTI scale is focusing on the assessment of brand and product evaluations, the concept of NFT is broader in scope and captures both an autotelic and an instrumental dimension. Autotelic NFT, on the one hand, is directed at the hedonic aspects of the touch experience. The construct measures the degree to which individuals describe touching objects as exciting and enjoyable and is thus also referred to as "funtouch" (Peck and Wiggins, 2006). Instrumental NFT, on the other hand, measures the more rational aspects of the touch experience. Consumer characterized by high levels of NFT typically use direct touch to gather relevant information about the object which they could not obtain through, e.g., verbal and visual cues (Peck and Childers, 2003b).

Related literature has demonstrated a variety of interaction effects between NFT and product characteristics. Peck and Childers (2003a) show that consumers high in NFT put more emphasis on material properties when evaluating products, thereby gathering haptic information. Another study examines the role of NFT on confidence in product judgment: while low-NFT subjects reported unchanged levels of judgment, high-NFT subjects felt increasingly uncomfortable and uncertain when unable to touch the product before making a purchase decision (Peck and Childers, 2003a). Grohmann et al. (2007) demonstrate that for consumers characterized by high NFT, tactile input can improve the ability to judge product quality and lead to more favorable object evaluations – especially when products possess many material attributes. Many subsequent studies confirmed the interaction of NFT with product and interface types (e.g., Brasel and Gips, 2014; Choi and Taylor, 2014).

Goal orientation. Consumer goals in online shopping have been dichotomized into searching for information retrieval and browsing for entertainment (Hoffman and Novak, 1996; Janiszewski, 1998). Correspondingly, Moe (2003) differentiates shopping strategies along two dimensions: purchasing horizon (immediate vs future) and search behavior (directed vs exploratory). While directed buying corresponds to the search for targeted information and represents a rather utilitarian dimension, exploratory search patterns drive casual browsing behavior and relate to hedonic utilities (e.g., Brucks, 1985). Both types can result in a subsequent purchase (Moe, 2003).

In the context of virtual product experience, Schlosser, (2003) highlights the role of individual goal differences in response to object interactivity. It is demonstrated that congruency between individual goals and interaction design can affect consumer attitudes: in particular, browsers hold more favorable attitudes when exposed to an object-interactive site. Searchers, in contrast, are more likely to be persuaded by information passively delivered through, e.g., direct to-the-point text blocks and static graphics. In a later study, Schlosser et al. (2006) examine the moderating effect of consumer goals with regard to online purchase decisions. Results suggest that effects of website investment and ability cannot be generalized to browsing-oriented consumers but are instead specific to search-oriented consumers. Browsers, in contrast, rely more on personal components providing higher levels of trust.

3.2.3.2 Individual Perceptions and Reactions

Perceived diagnosticity. The concept of perceived diagnosticity is rooted in studies on consumer trials of products and refers to the extent consumers consider certain shopping experiences helpful when evaluating products (Kempf and Smith, 1998). In the context of online shopping, Jiang and Benbasat (2005) define perceived diagnosticity as "the perceived ability of a Web interface to convey to customers relevant product information that helps them in understanding and evaluating the quality and performance of products sold online" (p. 117). As illustrated in subsequent studies, higher levels of perceived diagnosticity result in increased product understanding and enable more informed purchase decisions (Jiang and Benbasat, 2007a). However, it is important to distinguish between actual and perceived product understanding since convincing and compelling product experiences can sometimes lead to unrealistic expectations and clouded judgment of objective product performance (Jiang and Benbasat, 2007b; Hoch, 2002; Goodhue et al., 2000). A series of studies showed that 3D advertising (compared to conventional two-dimensional experiences) can increase consumers' perceived product knowledge and decision quality (Li et al., 2002). Following this rationale, Jiang and Benbasat (2005) demonstrate that higher levels of both visual and functional control (compared to static images) increase perceived diagnosticity for corresponding product attributes. Overmars and Poels (2015) build upon this work and provide a more granular perspective on such attributes and illustrate that image interactivity technology capable of simulating stroking gestures result in increased levels of perceived diagnosticity for experience attributes in particular. This relationship is shown to be mediated by visually induced tactile sensations.

Affective reaction. Ajzen (2001) reviews affect and cognition as competing antecedents of product evaluation. The expectancy-value model (Feather, 1982; Fishbein, 1963; Fishbein and Ajzen, 1975) suggests that evaluative judgments are an inevitable, effortless consequence of cognitive processes. In contrast, the affect-primacy hypothesis (Zajonc, 1980) ranks affect over cognition. Consequently, scholars have widely adopted a multi-component conceptualization which views both affect and cognition as essential determinants of attitude (Eagly and Chaiken, 1993; van der Pligt et al., 1997).In the following years, a similar development has taken place within the touch literature. Initially, most research on the persuasive effects of touch focused on the cognitive perspective. For instance, Schlosser (2003) demonstrates that object interactivity, if congruent with user goals, creates congruency and thus supports cognitive elaboration as well as more favorable attitudes. Peck and Wiggins (2006) argue that the persuasive effects of touch might go well beyond the provision of product information: in particular for consumers characterized by high levels of NFT, the enjoyment of touch interaction was found to increase affective reaction and persuasion. Ever since, many studies in the field of touch have embraced the cognitive-affective framework and integrated this view into research about the effects of visual and functional control mechanisms on consumer attitude, capturing both shopping enjoyment and perceived diagnosticity (e.g., Jiang and Benbasat, 2007a; Kim and Forsythe, 2008; Verhagen et al., 2014).

Mental simulation. The theory of grounded cognition suggests that our cognitive activity is generated using our bodily states, actions, and mental simulations (Barsalou, 2008). More specifically, it is proposed that all mental acts are linked to mental simulations triggered by modality-specific sensory experiences (e.g., Barsalou, 1999; Barsalou et al., 2003). Within this context, Richardson (1969) defines mental imagery as "all those quasi-sensory and quasi-perceptual experiences of which we are self-consciously aware, and which exist for us in the absence of those stimulus conditions that are known to produce their genuine sensory or perceptual counterparts, and which may be expected to have different consequences from their sensory or perceptual counterparts" (pp. 2–3). Mental simulation can be viewed as a more automatic form of such mental imagery, in a sense that exposure to virtual objects triggers the reenactment of multisensory experiences. Shen et al. (2016) illustrate this phenomenon using the example of a person eating a chocolate cake. Mere exposure to a related picture would trigger associated memories involving the smell, consistency and taste of the actual cake.

Schlosser (2003) was among the first to suggest that interacting with objects in the virtual world creates clearer mental imagery than if similar information is acquired passively – regardless of whether the user's goal was to search or to browse. The resulting mental simulation positively influences purchase intentions. Ever since, only few studies have further investigated the nature of sensory stimuli that produce mental simulation. Most prominently, Elder and Krishna (2012) propose a "visual depiction effect", which is built around the relationship between vision and motor simulation. Manipulating visual depiction (e.g., a picture showing a spoon at the left or right side in a soup), and handedness (left vs right), a match between product depiction and individual habits emerged as significant driver of embodied mental simulation and purchase intentions. Shen et al. (2016) in contrast, focus on the role of direct touch interfaces and argue that the act of directly reaching out to and interacting with an object displayed on a touchscreen is a much more direct metaphor for actual, physical touch than if the experience was mediated by peripheral devices such as a computer mouse, trackpad, or stylus. The resulting immediate touch response was shown to facilitate mental interaction, resulting in consumers favoring affect-laden products (such as a tasty chocolate cake) over a cognitively superior alternative (such as a rather healthy fruit salad). This phenomenon is referred to as the "direct touch effect".

Perceived user control. The perception of user control describes the degree consumers can modify their environment and is closely related to the concept of interactivity (Overmars and Poels, 2015; Klein, 2003; Steuer, 1992). The ability to directly experience products in brick-and-mortar stores is associated with high levels of control and feelings of "first-personness" through immediate feedback (Jiang and Benbasat, 2005; Hutchins et al., 1985) – an experience which is more difficult to replicate in mediated environments, such as electronic and mobile commerce settings. To create similar levels of customer engagement in the absence of physical control, an online browsing experience should be customizable to a degree that allows for active information selection and caters to basic informational customer needs (Lee et al., 2012; Liu and Shrum, 2002).

Peck et al. (2013) emphasize on the sense of touch as main mechanism through which consumers can manipulate objects. Building upon prior work establishing a relationship between object control and perceived ownership (Pierce et al., 2003; Peck and Shu, 2009; Shu and Peck, 2011), it is shown that touch and touch imagery result in greater perceived object control. In an online mediated environment, Overmars and Poels (2015) investigate the effects of directly manipulating an object though image interactivity as opposed to watching a video, indirectly showing a similar manipulation. Image interactive technologies, and thus higher levels of user control, lead to tactile sensations and in turn to high perceived diagnosticity of experience attributes.

Perceived ownership. The theoretical concept of ownership reaches well beyond legal claims. Children, for instance, tend to express subjective feelings of possession when they argue about objects they do not actually own (Furby, 1978; 1980). Pierce et al. (2001) studied a similar effect in to context of employees having feelings of ownership for their organization and coined the term "psychological ownership", which they define as "feeling of possessiveness and of being psychologically tied to an object" (p. 299). Similar types of anticipated possession have been demonstrated regarding several objects and options (Ariely and Simonson, 2003; Carmon et al., 2003). Throughout literature, the terms psychological ownership and perceived ownership are oftentimes used interchangeably.

Peck and Shu (2009) were the first to show that merely touching an object – in the absence of legal claims – increases perceived ownership. Through a replication of nine studies, Shu and Peck (2011) illustrate that touch is one of the central antecedents of perceived ownership, which in turn acts as consistent driver of object valuation. Taking abstraction one step further, Peck et al. (2013) investigate the effect of haptic imagery and vividness on perceived ownership. They find that feelings of possession are driven by increased perception of physical control, fueled by haptic imagery and vividness of the experience. Following this path, Brasel and Gips (2014) propose that reaching out to a product picture with one's hands much rather resembles touching the actual product than using an indirect interface such as a laptop's trackpad or a computer mouse. Hence, product exploration through digital touchscreens increases perceived ownership feelings and ultimately product endowment.

4   Research Agenda

Building upon the results of our systematic literature review, we develop a research agenda which outlines some of the major challenges in the research field of digital touch and discuss avenues for future research (Webster and Watson, 2002). Our structure is based on the combined approaches of Mahajan and Venkatesh (2000) as well as Parasuraman and Zinkhan (2002), differentiating between theory-, data-, method- and technology-related challenges.[2] The first three challenges are clustered according to our analytical framework, while technology-related challenges all relate to the digital interface. Table 6 summarizes the most pressing and prominent issues which could be addressed in future research. Please note that both the challenges and factors are, in part, strongly dependent on one another and are thus not mutually exclusive.

Table 6. Avenues for future research.

Category	Topic
Theory-related challenges	*Product-related factors* • Analysis of digital touch interaction with high and low involvement products *Interface-related factors* • Analysis of textural fit between interface and product surface • Analysis of virtual control mechanisms on mobile devices *Consumer-related factors* • Analysis of goal-oriented interface design
Data-related challenges	*Product-related factors* • Consideration of external product data such as competitor pricing *Interface-related factors* • Tracking of how (or, to which degree) virtual control mechanisms are used • Consideration of sensor data, such as eye-tracking *Consumer-related factors* • Collecting samples from all age groups, reflecting their different usage and adoption rates of mobile touch devices
Method-related challenges	*Product-related factors* • Control for product-brand awareness and its effects on consumer decisions with regard to product-level uncertainty *Interface-related factors* • Collection and analysis of field data across devices to control for prior product research and understand multichannel shopping behavior • Manipulation of interactivity, holding conveyed product information constant
Technology-related challenges	*Interface-related factors* • Limitations of interactive technologies and dynamic presentation formats in light of technical restrictions such as bandwidth or processing power • Consideration of advanced mobile interfaces and wearable devices • Consideration of augmented and virtual reality applications

---

[2] See Molitor (2015) and Dechant (2016) for a similar approach.

4.1   Theory-Related Challenges

Results of our literature review illustrate that there are a variety of product-, interface-
and consumer-related factors that influence the digital touch experience. Many of
these factors strongly influence one another, leading a to a high degree of complexity.
While it may be hard to generalize research findings and draw conclusions relevant to
all products or consumers, the recombination of factors allows for numerous research
opportunities still to be explored.

Product-related factors. In most laboratory studies, not more than one product-related
dimension is manipulated. As outlined by, e.g., Choi and Taylor (2014), it would be
interesting to learn whether findings regarding the digital product experience can be
replicated for products hedonic or utilitarian goods, service goods, or high vs. low
involvement goods. High involvement products in particular might require more than
just a single consumer touchpoint, oftentimes implying product research during a
longer time span and across multiple channels and devices. Here, future research at
the intersection between multichannel shopping and digital touch literature might hold
interesting insights into the role of virtual product experiences in the process of consumer decision-making.

Interface-related factors. Klatzky and Peck (2012) show that appealing product design and smooth surfaces trigger hedonic touch, while rough surface textures and increasing shape complexity were shown to be less inviting to touch and feel (Klatzky
and Peck, 2012). Within this context, Brasel and Gips (2014) propose examining the
effects of textural fit between the surfaces of a product and the touch interface: on
touchscreens, objects characterized by glass-like surfaces should feel superior compared to objects characterized by rough, bumpy textures. Hence, future research
should examine whether some products are, based on their surface texture, better
suited for exploration on touch devices than others. Moreover, it might be promising
to analyze virtual control mechanisms on mobile devices. Smartphones and tablets
have plenty of unique properties – among others touchscreen input, portability and
smaller screen sizes (e.g., Brasel and Gips, 2015; Ghose et al., 2013). The corresponding opportunities and restrictions could lead to substantial moderating effects of mobile devices when exploring the effects of visual and functional control mechanisms
on consumer behavior.

Consumer-related factors. Most user interfaces are guided by device-specific design,
e.g. responsive websites adapting to different screen sizes. Future studies could explore more consumer-specific interface designs, adapting to users' goal orientation
(i.e., to search, or to browse). For instance, Shen et al. (2016) argue that while traditional desktop PCs are most frequently used for more work-related tasks, tablets might
rather be used for leisure activities. Similarly, Xu et al. (2017) find that tablet PCs
spur hedonic browsing behavior. This line of work suggests that it might be promising
to design and study user interface adapting to consumer goals across device types.

4.2   Data-Related Challenges

Product-related factors. The majority of studies we analyzed has been conducted in the laboratory. Only two (De et al., 2013; Kim and Krishnan, 2015) out of 31 articles are based on field data. While large-scale observational datasets hold much more insights about real-life purchasing behavior, there are some caveats. For instance, competitor prices can be an omitted variable since many online shoppers compare prices and offerings across multiple websites. Hence, the decision to buy or not to buy can be substantially influenced by external market factors that are hard to control for. To mitigate this challenge, future studies could focus on market niches or products of subjective value, such as art. Furthermore, studies suggest that virtual control mechanisms influence consumers' willingness to pay (e.g., Roggeveen et al., 2015). Thus, it might be interesting to study online retailers who delegate price-setting to consumers.

Interface-related factors. When offering visual control mechanisms (such as zoom or alternative photo technology) or functional control mechanisms (such as interactive objects) on digital devices, it is oftentimes hard to measure if (or, how intensively) consumers made actual use of these opportunities (cf. De et al., 2013; Kim and Krishnan, 2015). Given the lack of empirical studies, as described above, data from field experiments which includes acceptance and usage frequency of interactive technologies could offer meaningful additional insights. Moreover, many mobile devices contain a variety of sensors which could provide a variety of additional data points.

Consumer-related factors. A large part of the analyzed studies relied on student samples. While this age group represents a major part of smartphone and tablet users, it should be considered that usage patterns and adoption rate of mobile devices substantially vary with age. There are separate, emerging literature streams focusing on toddlers (e.g., Bedford et al., 2016; Lovato and Waxman, 2016; Russo-Johnson et al., 2017) and seniors (e.g., Barnard et al., 2013; Hsiao et al., 2017; Tsai et al., 2017) interacting with mobile devices – however, to draw more generalizable conclusions, broader and more representative samples consisting of all age groups should be aspired.

4.3   Method-Related Challenges

Product-related factors. A major challenge when investigating the effects of haptic product experiences in the field, both online and offline, is to control for product-brand awareness. Exposure to commercials or a well-known brand could compensate for product-level uncertainty (Rao and Monroe, 1989) and thus lead to biased results. In particular when researching visual control mechanisms which influence consumer decisions through increased product information, brand-related effects should be taken into account. Furthermore, Kim and Krishnan (2015) suggest that purchase frequency for each product and across product categories should be considered to gain a better understanding of product-level uncertainty and its effect on purchase decisions.

Interface-related factors. Through mobile applications running on smartphones and tablets, online retailers have created additional touch points to reach out to their customers (Xu et al., 2017). In this regard, future empirical studies should strive for collecting field data across devices and device types to control for prior product research and understand multichannel shopping behavior. While datasets tracking user behavior through browser cookies would allow for session-specific choice modeling, log-in data from closed shopping ecosystems across devices could lead to valuable insights about user-specific purchasing behavior for an extended period of time. Another challenge is to measure unbiased effects of variations in virtual control mechanisms per se, in particular if the interactive format conveys additional product information (cf. De et al., 2013). Thus, it can be hard to hold product information constant and isolate, e.g., control- or gesture-specific interaction effects which can be attributed to certain static or dynamic presentation formats (cf. Roggeveen et al. (2015).

4.4   Technology-Related Challenges

The technology-related challenges affecting digital touch are primarily *interface-related*, i.e., centered around the mobile device mediating the digital product experience. Technology diffusion and adoption is a process of several years, which is why consumers tend to use a variety of different devices and contractual agreements with their internet service providers. This phenomenon is reinforced with product life-cycles shortening and smartphones being replaced after around 21 months on average (Statista, 2017). Many of the latest interactive technologies and dynamic presentation formats require certain minimum standards with regard to data volume, bandwidth, and processing power, and might therefore not be accessible to a large part of customers relying on mobile technology from previous generations. While retailers face the challenge of ensuring backward compatibility, researchers must find ways to account for heterogeneous device capabilities in the field.

From a hardware perspective, more and more computer-mediated interfaces are equipped with touch interfaces. Apple Inc., for instance, released laptop computers equipped with a multi-touch bar replacing the top row on keyboards. This way, users can use the bar for a variety of functions and use "Touch ID" to unlock the computer with their fingerprint instead of entering a password. Furthermore, "Force Touch" technology (also referred to as "3D Touch") has become part of Apple's computer trackpads, wearables, and iPhones (CNET, 2015). The technology is sensitive to pressure and enables multi-touch gestures so that the device can differentiate between different levels of force applied to the surface. Such technological advancements hold many new opportunities for refined haptic experiences on mobile devices (Heo and Lee, 2011). From a software perspective, a large number of augmented and virtual reality applications will become viable in the near future. Some retailers already experiment with, e.g., virtual mirror technology to create multisensory experiences (Verhagen et al., 2014). Virtual reality technology in particular could enable substantially higher levels of product visualization and real-time interaction (Altarteer et al., 2016).

5   Conclusion

With the rise of online shopping, retailers and scholars alike are presented with the challenge of how to compensate for product touch on computer-mediated interfaces. Over the past years, however, the rapid adoption of mobile touch devices such as smartphones and tablets created new opportunities to provide multisensory virtual product experiences. While the topic area of digital touch has attracted attention from various disciplines such as management, marketing, information systems and psychology, there is, to the best of our knowledge, no comprehensive literature review so far synthesizing findings from these different perspectives.

The contribution of this literature review is threefold: first, this work presents a systematic approach to identify, structure, and analyze relevant articles from the four disciplines mentioned above. Second, we map out and discuss product-, interface-, and consumer-related factors influencing the digital touch experience. Third, we develop a comprehensive agenda for future research that outlines some of the main theory-, data-, method- and technology-related challenges to be addressed in the coming years.

Our findings show that our research question is primarily addressed by marketing literature. Interestingly, however, a substantial part of considered articles published in 2014 or later stem from management and psychology literature, indicating rising interest from these disciplines. Within our sample, product-related factors are discussed least. This can be partly explained by the observation that the information systems and psychology literature we analyzed does not focus on product characteristics at all. Research on interface-related factors, however, is covered by all four disciplines. While studies in the 2000s emphasized on software-enabled interaction through visual and functional control mechanisms, more recent research has shifted the focus toward hardware enablers. Most prominently, the widespread adoption of mobile touch devices has triggered various opportunities to enhance and research the digital touch experience. Consumer-related factors are frequently discussed across disciplines as well. Many studies in the fields of marketing and psychology thereby focus on laboratory experiments to understand the underlying mental mechanisms. In contrast, field experiments and empirical datasets that observe actual consumer behavior are mainly used in management and information systems research.

While we considered several disciplines and journals, there might be additional research outside of our scope or selection criteria. Most notably, conference proceedings from human-computer interaction continuously explore technological advancements in interface design and conduct usability studies. Such findings could serve as inspiration for future research in the fields of business and psychology. To conclude, we share the perception of Shen et al. (2016) as well as Peck et al.(2013) that the literature on digital touch in consumer research is still in its infancy. This work provides an overview of driving factors to be further discussed, molded and recombined in future studies.

References

Adipat, B., Zhang, D., & Zhou, L. (2011). The Effects of Tree-View Based Presentation Adaption on Mobile Web Browsing. *MIS Quarterly, 35*(1), 99–122.

Ajzen, I. (2001). Nature and Operation of Attitudes. *Annual Review of Psychology, 52*(1), 27–58.

Alba, J., Lynch, J., Weitz, B., Janiszewski, C., Lutz, R., Sawyer, A., & Wood, S. (1997). Interactive Home Shopping: Consumer, Retailer, and Manufacturer Incentives to Participate in Electronic Marketplaces. *Journal of Marketing, 61*(3), 38.

Altarteer, S., Vassilis, C., Harrison, D., & Chan, W. (2016). Product Customization: Virtual Reality and New Opportunities for Luxury Brands Online Trading. In *Proceedings of the 21st International Conference on Web3D Technology - Web3D '16* (pp. 173–174). New York, New York, USA: ACM Press.

Ariely, D., & Simonson, I. (2003). Buying, Bidding, Playing, or Competing? Value Assessment and Decision Dynamics in Online Auctions. *Journal of Consumer Psychology, 13*(1–2), 113–123.

Barnard, Y., Bradley, M. D., Hodgson, F., & Lloyd, A. D. (2013). Learning to use new technologies by older adults: Perceived difficulties, experimentation behavior and usability. *Computers in Human Behavior, 29*(4), 1715–1724.

Barsalou, L. W. (1999). Perceptions of perceptual symbols. *Behavioral and Brain Sciences, 22*(4), 637–660.

Barsalou, L. W. (2008). Grounded Cognition. *Annual Review of Psychology, 59*(1), 617–645.

Barsalou, L. W., Simmons, W. K., Barbey, A. K., & Wilson, C. D. (2003). Grounding conceptual knowledge in modality-specific systems. *Trends in Cognitive Sciences.*

Bart, Y., Stephen, A. T., & Sarvary, M. (2014). Which Products Are Best Suited to Mobile Advertising? A Field Study of Mobile Display Advertising Effects on Consumer Attitudes and Intentions. *Journal of Marketing Research, 51*(3), 270–285.

Bedford, R., Saez de Urabain, I. R., Celeste, C. H., Karmiloff-Smith, A., & Smith, T. J. (2016). Toddlers' fine motor milestone achievement is associated with early touchscreen scrolling. *Frontiers in Psychology, 7*(8), 1–8.

Blazquez Cano, M., Perry, P., Ashman, R., & Waite, K. (2016). The influence of image interactivity upon user engagement when using mobile touch screens. *Computers in Human Behavior*, 1–7.

Bloch, P. H., & Richins, M. L. (1983). A Theoretical Model for the Study of Product Importance Perceptions. *Journal of Marketing, 47*(3), 69.

Bone, P. F., & Ellen, P. S. (1992). The Generation and Consequences of Communication-Evoked Imagery. *Journal of Consumer Research, 19*(1), 93.

Brasel, S. A., & Gips, J. (2014). Tablets, touchscreens, and touchpads: How varying touch interfaces trigger psychological ownership and endowment. *Journal of Consumer Psychology, 24*(2), 226–233.

Brasel, S. A., & Gips, J. (2015). Interface Psychology: Touchscreens Change Attribute Importance, Decision Criteria, and Behavior in Online Choice. *Cyberpsychology, Behavior, and Social Networking, 18*(9), 534–538.

Brucks, M. (1985). The Effects of Product Class Knowledge on Information Search Behavior. *Journal of Consumer Research, 12*(1), 1–16.

Burns, A. C., Biswas, A., & Babin, L. A. (1993). The Operation of Visual Imagery as a Mediator of Advertising Effects. *Journal of Advertising, 22*(2), 71–85.

Carmon, Z., Wertenbroch, K., & Zeelenberg, M. (2003). Option Attachment: When Deliberating Makes Choosing Feel like Losing. *Journal of Consumer Research, 30*(1), 15–29.

Childers, T. L., Carr, C. L., Peck, J., & Carson, S. (2001). Hedonic and utilitarian motivations for online retail shopping behavior. *Journal of Retailing, 77*(4), 511–535.

Childers, T. L., Houston, M. J., & Heckler, S. E. (1985). Measurement of Individual Differences in Visual versus Verbal Information Processing. *Journal of Consumer Research, 12*(2), 125.

Choi, Y. K., & Taylor, C. R. (2014). How do 3-dimensional images promote products on the Internet? *Journal of Business Research, 67*(10), 2164–2170.

Citrin, A. V., Stem, D. E., Spangenberg, E. R., & Clark, M. J. (2003). Consumer need for tactile input: An internet retailing challenge. *Journal of Business Research, 56*(11), 915–922.

CNET. (2015). How Apple's Force Touch could change the way you use your next iPhone or iPad. Retrieved September 7, 2017, from https://www.cnet.com/news/what-force-touch-could-do-for-the-next-iphones-and-ipads/.

Coyle, J. R., & Thorson, E. (2001). The Effects of Progressive Levels of Interactivity and Vividness in Web Marketing Sites. *Journal of Advertising, 30*(3), 65–77.

De, P., Hu, Y. (Jeffrey), & Rahman, M. S. (2013). Product-Oriented Web Technologies and Product Returns: An Exploratory Study. *Information Systems Research, 24*(4), 998–1010.

Dechant, A. (2016). *Customer Behavior in Online Dating*. Books on Demand, Norderstedt; zugl. Dissertation, Ludwig-Maximilians-Universität München.

Degeratu, A. M., Rangaswamy, A., & Wu, J. (2000). Consumer choice behavior in online and traditional supermarkets: The effects of brand name, price, and other search attributes. *International Journal of Research in Marketing, 17*(1), 55–78.

Dhar, R., & Wertenbroch, K. (2000). Consumer Choice Between Hedonic and Utilitarian Goods. *Journal of Marketing Research, 37*(1), 60–71.

Dimoka, A., Hong, Y., & Pavlou, P. A. (2012). On Product Uncertainty in Online Markets: Theory and Evidence. *MIS Quarterly, 36*(2), 395–426.

Eagly, A. H., & Chaiken, S. (1993). *The psychology of attitudes*. Harcourt Brace Jovanovich College.

Elder, R. S., & Krishna, A. (2012). The "Visual Depiction Effect" in Advertising: Facilitating Embodied Mental Simulation through Product Orientation. *Journal of Consumer Research, 38*(6), 988–1003.

Feather, N. (1982). *Expectations and actions: Expectancy-value models in psychology*. Lawrence Erlbaum Associates.

Fiore, A. M., & Jin, H. (2003). Influence of image interactivity on approach responses towards an online retailer. *Internet Research, 13*(1), 38–48.

Fiore, A. M., Kim, J., & Lee, H.-H. (2005). Effect of image interactivity technology on consumer responses toward the online retailer. *Journal of Interactive Marketing, 19*(3), 38–53.

Fishbein, M. (1963). An Investigation of the Relationships between Beliefs about an Object and the Attitude toward that Object. *Human Relations, 16*(3), 233–239.

Fishbein, M., & Ajzen, I. (1975). Belief, attitude, intention and behavior: An introduction to theory and research.

Furby, L. (1978). Possession in Humans: An Exploratory Study of Its Meaning and Motivation. *Social Behavior and Personality, 6*(1), 49–65.

Furby, L. (1980). The Origins and Early Development of Possessive Behavior. *Political Psychology, 2*(1), 30–42.

Ghose, A., Goldfarb, A., & Han, S. P. (2013). How is the mobile internet different? Search costs and local activities. *Information Systems Research, 24*(3), 613–631.

Goodhue, D. L., Klein, B. D., & March, S. T. (2000). User Evaluations of IS as Surrogates for Objective Performance. *Information & Management, 38*(2), 87–101.

Grewal, D., Bart, Y., Spann, M., & Zubcsek, P. P. (2016). Mobile Advertising: A Framework and Research Agenda. *Journal of Interactive Marketing, 34*, 3–14.

Grohmann, B., Spangenberg, E. R., & Sprott, D. E. (2007). The influence of tactile input on the evaluation of retail product offerings. *Journal of Retailing, 83*(2), 237–245.

Hein, W., O'Donohoe, S., & Ryan, A. (2011). Mobile phones as an extension of the participant observer's self. *Qualitative Market Research: An International Journal, 14*(3), 258–273.

Heo, S., & Lee, G. (2011). Force Gestures: Augmenting Touch Screen Gestures with Normal and Tangential Forces. *Proceedings of the 24th Annual ACM Symposium on User Interface Software and Technology - UIST '11*, 621–626.

Hoch, S. J. (2002). Product Experience Is Seductive. *Journal of Consumer Research, 29*(3), 448–454.

Hoffman, D. L., & Novak, T. P. (1996). Marketing in Hypermedia Environment Foundations: Conceptual Foundations. *Journal of Marketing, 60*(3), 50–68. https://doi.org/10.2307/1251841

Hsiao, S.-W., Lee, C.-H., Yang, M.-H., & Chen, R.-Q. (2017). User interface based on natural interaction design for seniors. *Computers in Human Behavior, 75*, 147–159.

Hutchins, E., Hollan, J., & Norman, D. (1985). Direct Manipulation Interfaces. *Human-Computer Interaction, 1*(4), 311–338.

Janiszewski, C. (1998). The Influence of Display Characteristics on Visual Exploratory Search Behavior. *Journal of Consumer Research, 25*(3), 290–301.

Jesson, J., Matheson, L., & Lacey, F. M. (2011). *Doing Your Literature Review.* SAGE Publications.

Jiang, Z., & Benbasat, I. (2005). Virtual Product Experience: Effects of Visual and Functional Control of Products on Perceived Diagnosticity and Flow in Electronic Shopping. *Journal of Management Information Systems, 21*(3), 111–147.

Jiang, Z., & Benbasat, I. (2007a). Investigating the Influence of the Functional Mechanisms of Online Product Presentations. *Information Systems Research, 18*(4), 454–470.

Jiang, Z., & Benbasat, I. (2007b). The Effects of Presentation Formats and Task Complexity on Online Consumers' Product Understanding. *MIS Quarterly, 31*(3), 497–520.

Jin, S. A. A. (2009). The Roles of Modality Richness and Involvement in Shopping Behavior in 3D Virtual Stores. *Journal of Interactive Marketing, 23*(3), 234–246.

Kempf, D. S., & Smith, R. E. (1998). Consumer Processing of Product Trial and the Influence of Prior Advertising: A Structural Modeling Approach. *Journal of Marketing Research, 35*(3), 325.

Kim, J., & Forsythe, S. (2008). Adoption of Virtual Try-on technology for online apparel shopping. *Journal of Interactive Marketing, 22*(2), 45–59.

Kim, Y., & Krishnan, R. (2015). On Product-Level Uncertainty and Online Purchase Behavior: An Empirical Analysis. *Management Science, 61*(10), 2449–2467.

Klatzky, R. L., & Lederman, S. J. (1993). Toward a Computational Model of Constraint-Driven Exploration and Haptic Object Identification. *Perception, 22*(5), 597–621.

Klatzky, R. L., Lederman, S. J., & Matula, D. E. (1993). Haptic exploration in the presence of vision. *Journal of Experimental Psychology. Human Perception and Performance.*

Klatzky, R. L., & Peck, J. (2012). Please Touch: Object Properties that Invite Touch. *IEEE Transactions on Haptics, 5*(2), 139–147.

Klein, L. R. (2003). Creating virtual product experiences: The role of telepresence. *Journal of Interactive Marketing, 17*(1), 41–55.

Kotler, P., & Bloom, P. (1984). *Marketing professional services: forward-thinking strategies for boosting your business, your image, and your profits.* Prentice Hall Press.

Lal, R., & Sarvary, M. (1999). When and How is the Internet Likely to Decrease Price Competition? *Marketing Science, 18*(4), 485–503.

Laroche, M., Bergeron, J., & Goutaland, C. (2001). A Three-Dimensional Scale of Intangibility. *Journal of Service Research, 4*(1), 26–38.

Laroche, M., Yang, Z., McDougall, G. H. G., & Bergeron, J. (2005). Internet versus bricks-and-mortar retailers: An investigation into intangibility and its consequences. *Journal of Retailing, 81*(4), 251–267.

Lederman, S. J., & Klatzky, R. L. (1987). Hand movements: A window into haptic object recognition. *Cognitive Psychology, 19*(3), 342–368.

Lederman, S. J., & Klatzky, R. L. (1990). Haptic classification of common objects: Knowledge-driven exploration. *Cognitive Psychology, 22*(4), 421–459.

Lee, B., Isenberg, P., Riche, N. H., & Carpendale, S. (2012). Beyond mouse and keyboard: Expanding design considerations for information visualization interactions. *IEEE Transactions on Visualization and Computer Graphics*, *18*(12), 2689–2698.

Li, H., Daugherty, T., & Biocca, F. (2002). Impact of 3-D Advertising on Product Knowledge, Brand Attitude, and Purchase Intention: The Mediating Role of Presence. *Journal of Advertising*, *31*(3), 43–57.

Liu, Y., & Shrum, L. J. (2002). What is Interactivity and is it Always Such a Good Thing? Implications of Definition, Person, and Situation for the Influence of Interactivity on Advertising Effectiveness. *Journal of Advertising*, *31*(4), 53–64.

Lorenz, D., & Löffler, A. (2015). Robustness of personal rankings: the Handelsblatt example. *Business Research*, *8*(2), 189–212.

Lovato, S. B., & Waxman, S. R. (2016). Young children learning from touch screens: Taking a wider view. *Frontiers in Psychology*, *7*(JUL), 1–6.

Lynch, J. G., & Ariely, D. (2000). Wine Online: Search Costs Affect Competition on Price, Quality, and Distribution. *Marketing Science*, *19*(1), 83–103.

Mahajan, V., & Venkatesh, R. (2000). Marketing modeling for e-business. *International Journal of Research in Marketing*, *17*(2–3), 215–225.

Mayring, P. (2014). *Qualitative Content Analysis Theoretical Foundation, Basic Procedures and Software Solution.*

McCabe, D. B., & Nowlis, S. M. (2003). The Effect of Examining Actual Products or Product Descriptions on Consumer Preference. *Journal of Consumer Psychology*, *13*(4), 431–439.

McDougall, G. H. G., & Snetsinger, D. W. (1990). The intangibility of services: Measurement and competitive perspectives. *Journal of Services Marketing*, *4*(4), 27–40.

Moe, W. W. (2003). Buying, Searching, or Browsing: Differentiating Between Online Shoppers Using In-Store Navigational Clickstream. *Journal of Consumer Psychology*, *13*(2000), 29–39.

Molitor, D. (2015). *Location-Based Advertising: Context and Consumer Behavior.* epubli Verlag, Berlin; zugl. Dissertation, Ludwig-Maximilians-Universität München.

Mooy, S. C., & Robben, H. S. J. (2002). Managing consumers' product evaluations through direct product experience. *Journal of Product & Brand Management*, *11*(7), 432–446.

Nelson, P. (1970). Information and Consumer Behavior. *Journal of Political Economy*, *78*(2), 311–329.

Nelson, P. (1974). Advertising as Information. *Journal of Political Economy*, *82*(4), 729–754.

Nisbett, R. E., & Ross, L. (1980). Assigning weights to data: The "vividness criterion." In R. E. Nisbett & L. Ross (Eds.), *Human Inference: Strategies and Shortcomings of Social Judgment.* Prentice-Hall.

Overmars, S., & Poels, K. (2015). Online product experiences: The effect of simulating stroking gestures on product understanding and the critical role of user control. *Computers in Human Behavior*, *51*(PA), 272–284.

Parasuraman, A., & Zinkhan, G. M. (2002). Marketing to and Serving Customers through the Internet: An Overview and Research Agenda. *Journal of the Academy of Marketing Science, 30*(4), 286–295.

Peck, J., Barger, V. A., & Webb, A. (2013). In search of a surrogate for touch: The effect of haptic imagery on perceived ownership. *Journal of Consumer Psychology, 23*(2), 189–196.

Peck, J., & Childers, T. L. (2003a). Individual Differences in Haptic Information Processing: The "Need for Touch" Scale. *Journal of Consumer Research, 30*(3), 430–442.

Peck, J., & Childers, T. L. (2003b). To Have and To Hold: The Influence of Haptic Information on Product Judgments. *Journal of Marketing, 67*(2), 35–48.

Peck, J., & Shu, S. B. (2009). The Effect of Mere Touch on Perceived Ownership. *Journal of Consumer Research, 36*(3), 434–447.

Peck, J., & Wiggins, J. (2006). It Just Feels Good: Customers' Affective Response to Touch and Its Influence on Persuasion. *Journal of Marketing, 70*(4), 56–69.

Pierce, J. L., Kostova, T., & Dirks, K. T. (2001). Toward a Theory of Psychological Ownership in Organizations. *Academy of Management Review, 26*(2), 298–310.

Pierce, J. L., Kostova, T., & Dirks, K. T. (2003). The state of psychological ownership: Integrating and extending a century of research. *Review of General Psychology, 7*(1), 84–107.

Richardson, A. (1969). *Mental Imagery*. Springer.

Roggeveen, A. L., Grewal, D., Townsend, C., & Krishnan, R. (2015). The Impact of Dynamic Presentation Format on Consumer Preferences for Hedonic Products and Services. *Journal of Marketing, 79*(6), 34–49.

Rudmin, F. W., & Berry, J. W. (1987). Semantics of Ownership: A Free-Recall Study of Property. *The Psychological Record, 37*(2), 257–268.

Russo-Johnson, C., Troseth, G., Duncan, C., & Mesghina, A. (2017). All Tapped Out: Touchscreen Interactivity and Young Children's Word Learning. *Frontiers in Psychology, 8*(April), 1–15.

Schlosser, A. E. (2003). Experiencing Products in the Virtual World: The Role of Goal and Imagery in Influencing Attitudes versus Purchase Intentions. *Journal of Consumer Research, 30*(2), 184–198.

Schlosser, A. E. (2006). Learning through Virtual Product Experience: The Role of Imagery on True versus False Memories. *Journal of Consumer Research, 33*(3), 377–383.

Schlosser, A. E., White, T. B., & Lloyd, S. M. (2006). Converting Web Site Visitors into Buyers: How Web Site Investment Increases Consumer Trusting Beliefs and Online Purchase Intentions. *Journal of Marketing, 70*(2), 133–148.

Schrader, U., & Hennig-Thurau, T. (2009). VHB-JOURQUAL2: Method, Results, and Implications of the German Academic Association for Business Research's Journal Ranking. *Business Research, 2*(2), 180–204.

Shen, H., Zhang, M., & Krishna, A. (2016). Computer Interfaces and the "Direct-Touch" Effect: Can iPads Increase the Choice of Hedonic Food? *Journal of Marketing Research, 53*(5), 745–758.

Sherman, S. J., Mackie, D. M., & Driscoll, D. M. (1990). Priming and the Differential Use of Dimensions in Evaluation. *Personality and Social Psychology Bulletin, 16*(3), 405–418.

Shneiderman, B. (1987). User Interface Design for the Hyperties Electronic Encyclopedia. In *1987 ACM Conference on Hypertext* (pp. 189–194). ACM Press.

Shu, S. B., & Peck, J. (2011). Psychological ownership and affective reaction: Emotional attachment process variables and the endowment effect. *Journal of Consumer Psychology, 21*(4), 439–452.

Statista. (2017). Smartphone Life Cycles Are Changing. Retrieved September 7, 2017, from https://www.statista.com/chart/8348/smartphone-life-cycles-are-changing/.

Steuer, J. (1992). Defining Virtual Reality: Dimensions Determining Telepresence. *Journal of Communication, 42*(4), 73–93.

Tsai, T.-H., Tseng, K. C., & Chang, Y.-S. (2017). Testing the usability of smartphone surface gestures on different sizes of smartphones by different age groups of users. *Computers in Human Behavior, 75*, 103–116.

van der Pligt, J., Zeelenberg, M., van Dijk, W. W., de Vries, N. K., & Richard, R. (1997). Affect, Attitudes and Decisions: Let's Be More Specific. *European Review of Social Psychology, 8*(1), 33–66

Verhagen, T., Vonkeman, C., Feldberg, F., & Verhagen, P. (2014). Computers in Human Behavior Present it like it is here: Creating local presence to improve online product experiences. *Computers in Human Behavior, 39*, 270–280.

Webster, J., & Watson, R. T. (2002). Analyzing the past to prepare for the future: Writing a literature review. *MIS Quarterly, 26*(2), xiii–xxiii.

Xu, K., Chan, J., Ghose, A., & Han, S. P. (2017). Battle of the Channels: The Impact of Tablets on Digital Commerce. *Management Science, 63*(5), 1469–1492.

Zajonc, R. B. (1980). Feeling and thinking: Preferences need no inferences. *American Psychologist, 35*(2), 151–175.

Appendix

A1. Overview of Journals in the Literature Review (Based on VHB-JOURQUAL 3 and Ranked by Overall Rating Score)

Journal	VHB JQ3	Subcategory
Science	A+	Management
American Economic Review	A+	Management
Econometrica	A+	Management
Academy of Management Journal	A+	Management
Journal of Political Economy	A+	Management
Administrative Science Quarterly	A+	Management
Academy of Management Review	A+	Management
Management Science	A+	Management
Strategic Management Journal	A	Management
The RAND Journal of Economics	A	Management
Journal of Industrial Economics	A	Management
Experimental Economics	A	Management
Academy of Management Annals	A	Management
Journal of Management	A	Management
Journal of Management Studies	A	Management
Journal of Economics & Management Strategy	A	Management
Organization Studies	A	Management
Journal of Economic Psychology	B	Management
Omega	B	Management
Long Range Planning	B	Management
Journal of Business Research	B	Management
International Journal of Industrial Organization	B	Management
British Journal of Management	B	Management
Schmalenbach Business Review	B	Management
Journal of Business Economics	B	Management

Journal	VHB JQ3	Subcategory
Journal of Management Inquiry	B	Management
International Review of Law and Economics	B	Management
Review of Managerial Science	B	Management
Kyklos	B	Management
Academy of Management Perspectives	B	Management
Business Research	B	Management
International Journal of Management Reviews	B	Management
Journal of Behavioral and Experimental Economics	B	Management
Qualitative Research in Accounting & Management	B	Management
European Management Journal	B	Management
Journal of Management Education	B	Management
Scandinavian Journal of Management	B	Management
California Management Review	B	Management
Journal of Marketing Research	A+	Marketing
Journal of Marketing	A+	Marketing
Journal of Consumer Research	A+	Marketing
Marketing Science	A+	Marketing
Journal of Applied Psychology	A	Marketing
International Journal of Research in Marketing	A	Marketing
Journal of the Academy of Marketing Science	A	Marketing
Journal of Retailing	A	Marketing
Journal of Service Research	A	Marketing
Journal of Product Innovation Management	A	Marketing
Journal of Consumer Psychology	A	Marketing
Marketing Letters	B	Marketing
Journal of International Marketing	B	Marketing
Decision Support Systems	B	Marketing
Quantitative Marketing and Economics	B	Marketing

Journal	VHB JQ3	Subcategory
Journal of Interactive Marketing	B	Marketing
Psychology & Marketing	B	Marketing
Journal of Behavioral Decision Making	B	Marketing
Journal of Forecasting	B	Marketing
Structural Equation Modeling: A Multidisciplinary Journal	B	Marketing
Journal of Cultural Economics	B	Marketing
Journal of Communication	B	Marketing
Journal of Public Policy & Marketing	B	Marketing
Group Decision and Negotiation	B	Marketing
Journal of Media Economics	B	Marketing
AMS Review	B	Marketing
Journal of Advertising	B	Marketing
Journal of Personal Selling & Sales Management	B	Marketing
Journal of Purchasing & Supply Management	B	Marketing
Industrial Marketing Management	B	Marketing
International Marketing Review	B	Marketing
Journal of Service Management	B	Marketing
Information Systems Research	A+	Information Systems
Management Information Systems Quarterly	A+	Information Systems
Journal of Management Information Systems	A	Information Systems
Mathematical Programming	A	Information Systems
Journal of the Association for Information Systems	A	Information Systems
Journal of Information Technology	A	Information Systems
Proceedings of the Internat. Conference on Information Systems	A	Information Systems
Information Systems Journal	A	Information Systems
The Journal of Strategic Information Systems	A	Information Systems
European Journal of Information Systems	A	Information Systems
INFORMS Journal on Computing	A	Information Systems

Journal	VHB JQ3	Subcategory
SIAM Journal on Computing	A	Information Systems
Journal of the ACM	B	Information Systems
Decision Support Systems	B	Information Systems
Decision Sciences	B	Information Systems
Computers and Operations Research	B	Information Systems
IEEE Transactions on Engineering Management	B	Information Systems
Business & Information Systems Engineering	B	Information Systems
ACM Transactions on Information Systems	B	Information Systems
International Journal of Electronic Commerce	B	Information Systems
ACM Transactions on Management Information Systems	B	Information Systems
ACM Computing Surveys	B	Information Systems
Journal of Computational Finance	B	Information Systems
Artificial Intelligence	B	Information Systems
Group Decision and Negotiation	B	Information Systems
ACM SIGMIS Database	B	Information Systems
Proceedings of the European Conference on Information Systems	B	Information Systems
IEEE Transactions on Software Engineering	B	Information Systems
Data & Knowledge Engineering	B	Information Systems
Proceedings of the Internat. Conference on Conceptual Modeling	B	Information Systems
Communications of the ACM	B	Information Systems
Information & Management	B	Information Systems
Information Systems	B	Information Systems
MIS Quarterly Executive	B	Information Systems
Journal of Decision Systems	B	Information Systems
Information and Organization	B	Information Systems
Information Systems Frontiers	B	Information Systems
Electronic Markets	B	Information Systems
ACM Transactions on Computer-Human Interaction	B	Information Systems

A2. Overview of Journals in the Literature Review (Based on and Ranked Impact Factor)

Journal	Impact Factor	Subcategory
Psychological Science in the Public Interest	19.286	Multidisciplinary Psychology
Annual Review of Psychology	19.085	Multidisciplinary Psychology
Psychological Bulletin	14.839	Multidisciplinary Psychology
Perspectives on Psychological Science	7.658	Multidisciplinary Psychology
Psychological Review	7.581	Multidisciplinary Psychology
Psychological Inquiry	6.714	Multidisciplinary Psychology
Current Directions in Psychological Science	5.545	Multidisciplinary Psychology
Journal of Abnormal Psychology	5.538	Multidisciplinary Psychology
Psychological Science	5.476	Multidisciplinary Psychology
American Psychologist	5.454	Multidisciplinary Psychology
Psychological Methods	5.000	Multidisciplinary Psychology
Emotion Review	4.730	Multidisciplinary Psychology
Annals of Behavioral Medicine	4.195	Multidisciplinary Psychology
Psychosomatic Medicine	3.638	Multidisciplinary Psychology
Neurobiology of Learning and Memory	3.439	Multidisciplinary Psychology
European Psychologist	3.372	Multidisciplinary Psychology
Behavior Genetics	3.268	Multidisciplinary Psychology
Psycho-Oncology	3.256	Multidisciplinary Psychology
Intelligence	3.118	Multidisciplinary Psychology
Environment and Behavior	2.892	Multidisciplinary Psychology
Computers in Human Behavior	2.880	Multidisciplinary Psychology
Journal of Gerontology Series B-Psychological Sciences and Social Sciences	2.813	Multidisciplinary Psychology
Psychology of Addictive Behaviors	2.780	Multidisciplinary Psychology
Journal of Gambling Studies	2.750	Multidisciplinary Psychology
Suicide and Life-Threating Behavior	2.726	Multidisciplinary Psychology
Journal of Environmental Psychology	2.647	Multidisciplinary Psychology
Journal of Comparative Psychology	2.494	Multidisciplinary Psychology

Aggressive Behavior	2.469	Multidisciplinary Psychology
Frontiers in Psychology	2.463	Multidisciplinary Psychology
Psychology of Women Quarterly	2.397	Multidisciplinary Psychology
British Journal of Psychology	2.243	Multidisciplinary Psychology
Body Image	2.104	Multidisciplinary Psychology
American Journal of Community Psychology	2.068	Multidisciplinary Psychology

III   Article 2

Quantified UX: Towards a Common Organizational Understanding of User Experience[1]

Abstract

User Experience (UX) is increasingly being recognized as an important factor for the commercial success of digital products. In fact, it has become a buzzword, which is interpreted differently by different parties. This lack of common understanding inevitably leads to misunderstandings and inefficiency in industrial practice. We therefore propose a quantifiable way of describing User Experience (QUX). Based on the analysis of 84 UX evaluation methods, a sample of UX characteristics from literature, and 24 interviews with experts from academia and practice, we propose a formalism and a corresponding tool to measure, visualize, and communicate a product's UX within organizations. We showcase the benefits of our approach by integrating it into the product development processes of companies from three different industries.

Keywords: *user experience; evaluation; interdisciplinary teams*

[1] This article is based on the following publication: Lachner, F., Naegelein, P., Kowalski, R., Spann, M., & Butz, A. (2016). Quantified UX: Towards a Common Organizational Understanding of User Experience. *Proceedings of the 9th Nordic Conference on Human-Computer Interaction.* ACM.

1   Introduction

With increasing maturity of an industry, usability is more and more taken for granted (Pine and Gilmore, 1998). Pleasurable and hedonic product attributes are at least as important as pragmatic product attributes for commercial success and customer loyalty (Alves et al., 2014; Battarbee and Koskinen, 2005). Hence, it is not surprising that the concept of User Experience (UX) is widely discussed within the Human-Computer Interaction (HCI) community, among both academics and industry practitioners. Still, UX has remained a buzzword that is much rather used as a collective term for investigating the quality-in-use of interactive products (Hassenzahl, 2008; Law et al., 2009). Furthermore, there is a variety of additional stakeholders with diverse perspectives involved in the creation of a product's UX (Alves et al., 2014; Hellman and Rönkkö, 2008).

In this paper, we present the development of a tool that aims to support a common organizational understanding of a product's UX and the selection of further in-depth UX evaluations. Against this background, it is crucial to understand the role that UX plays in the process of product development. Traditionally, a company's product development has been structured as follows. First, user researchers and psychologists identify user needs and UX objectives. Second, designers and engineers translate these goals into product features and their design characteristics. Third, experts in marketing and branding define advertising messages to convey the respective experience (Jordan, 1998; Väänänen-Vainio-Mattila et al., 2008). Finally, product managers incorporate the UX goals in the business context. Ideally, these steps are not separated from one another but strongly interlinked to ensure a holistic and consistent UX (Hellman and Rönkkö, 2008).

To create a certain UX, a systematic approach and an associated description of UX are needed to consider and measure the intended experience. Within this context, professionals demand a UX description that contains relevant criteria to support a transfer of UX into industrial practice. Existing development and design methods, however, rarely cope with the required degree of interdisciplinarity to reflect the different angles of e.g. engineering, design, marketing, or psychology (Cooper et al., 2014; Law et al., 2009). In the following sections, we will discuss the roles relevant for and the disciplines involved in the creation and improvement of a product's UX as part of design processes. Our goal is to address the following research question: How can we help organizations to measure, visualize, and communicate a product's UX within interdisciplinary teams?

This paper offers two main contributions: First, we propose a specific, quantifiable way of describing user experience, which we call quantified UX (QUX). Second, we develop a graphical tool that connects these UX characteristics with associated disciplines in a visually appealing way to support the compact communication of UX goals within an organization.

2   Theoretical Background

2.1   User Experience Research

After several years of UX research, scholars seem to have reached consensus with regard to experience-oriented concepts that exceed traditional functionality and usability considerations (Hassenzahl and Tractinsky, 2006). UX evaluation ranges from the analysis of psychological needs to task-oriented user goals or guidelines (Alves et al., 2014). The satisfaction of human needs is seen as a driver of experiences (Sheldon et al., 2001). However, the consideration of such psychological needs is rather suitable for a *macro perspective*, i.e., the product's overall purpose. For the evaluation of a product on the market, a rather focused *micro perspective* on specific product characteristics, i.e., visceral characteristics, should be analyzed in detail (Hassenzahl, 2008; Norman, 2013). We argue that it is inevitable for a practically oriented UX evaluation and communication process in interdisciplinary teams to narrow down the broad scope of UX to a quantifiable level. Therefore, we base our research on the concept of product-oriented user goals and define UX as the result of enjoyable interactions and/or anticipated interactions with a product.

Different perceptions of UX are not limited to academia. Many newcomers to the field of UX, and a large number of UX practitioners, struggle with the complexity and vague definition of UX as well (Gray, 2014). Furthermore, industry practitioners are presented with another challenge: to cope with the inability to talk to users directly while they interact with their product, as (prototype) workshops or laboratory experiments are often cost-intensive and time-consuming. Interdisciplinary project settings may increase the level of complexity even further.

To achieve the intended UX, a large variety of different UX tools and methods are used along the distinct phases of product development processes (Väänänen-Vainio-Mattila et al., 2008b). In general, organizations are thereby particularly interested in long-term UX as they want to foster a positive overall experience rather than focus on temporary emotions (Law et al., 2009). Most academic researchers concentrate on investigating UX from a theoretical perspective. Industry practitioners, in contrast, need tools and methods that make UX assessable and manageable. As a consequence, it has remained a challenge to close this gap between theory and practice (Väänänen-Vainio-Mattila et al., 2008b).

2.2   Existing UX Evaluation Methods

Traditionally, research and development (R&D) departments focused their user research and product testing on usability requirements and quantitative methods, whereas marketing and advertising departments were responsible for communicating a certain experience (Väänänen-Vainio-Mattila et al., 2008b). However, along with a shift from a usability-focused to an experience-oriented perspective on product interactions, a shift within evaluation methodologies seems to have taken place (Bargas-Avila and Hornbæk, 2011).

The aforementioned gap between academic and practical interpretations of UX leads to substantial differences in the question of how UX should be evaluated (Väänänen-Vainio-Mattila et al., 2008b). First, user researchers typically disentangle evaluation processes from metric-based methods and focus on qualitative data in order to evaluate UX. However, the practicability of such methods is comparably low since the analysis of associated data may be hard and time-consuming. Thus, organizations and UX practitioners need evaluation tools which are quick to use and provide validated UX measures (Hellman and Rönkkö, 2008; Vermeeren et al., 2010). Second, since UX evaluation is usually considered costly, UX research often addresses evaluation methodologies for early product stages to identify requirements as early as possible. In industrial practice, however, UX evaluation is mainly pursued to improve and refine existing products (Alves et al., 2014; Burmester et al., 2010; Väänänen-Vainio-Mattila et al., 2008).

Against this background, we analyzed 84 UX evaluation tools from *http://www.allaboutux.org* (Roto et al., 2015), a collection of tools of a holistic study of UX measuring methods used in academia and industry (Vermeeren et al., 2010). In general, the landscape of UX evaluation offers a wide variety of tools and methods. From the viewpoint of an organization and its interdisciplinary product teams however, we conjecture that it is still hard to measure, visualize, and communicate a product's intended UX. In order to deduce requirements that meet the needs of interdisciplinary teams we examined the focus of the 84 UX evaluation tools from Roto et al. (2015). Thus, we were able to identify requirements for an interdisciplinary QUX approach based on five different evaluation clusters:

1. Measuring Sensation. A range of methods, such as *Emocards, Emofaces,* as well as *PrEmo* (Desmet, 2004) overcome the intangibility of measuring emotions by substituting verbal measurement dimensions with cartoons. Evaluators describe their experiences of using a product by choosing one out of a number of predefined cartoons. Furthermore, *FaceReader* (Den Uyl and van Kuilenburg, 2005) is a tool that automatically tracks facial expressions of users or evaluators. With a focus on feelings and sensation, pragmatic characteristics recede in the background of UX evaluation. For QUX, however, we want to focus on both hedonic and pragmatic product characteristics.

2. Specific Use Case. Further methods focus on a specific use case, e.g., a specific product or feature: The *Aesthetics scale* (Lavie and Tractinsky, 2004) helps to evaluate websites, whereas the *Perceived Comfort Assessment* (Helander and Zhang, 1997) is a method of measuring the comfort level of, e.g., car seats. In contrast, we want to ensure the applicability of our QUX approach for various types of products.

3. Extensive Analysis. The *Experience Sampling Method (ESM;* Scollon et al., 2003) asks participants at certain times during the day to take notes about their current experiences. The *Outdoor Play Observation Scheme* (Bakker et al., 2008) integrates video recording to analyze children's' experiences with outdoor games. Both methods indicate the time-consuming analysis of UX evaluations. However, fast- paced industry projects generally require cost-efficient evaluation methods (Väänänen-Vainio-Mattila et al., 2008a).

4. Qualitative Evaluation. The *Day Reconstruction Method (DRM;* Karapanos et al., 2009) is a self-report method where participants note experiences in form of a diary. The *UX Curve* (Kujala et al., 2011) or *iScale* (Karapanos et al., 2010) measure the quality of an experience over time. Thereby, researchers understand when and how an experience changed but cannot easily analyze why a certain experience was formed or triggered.

5. Questionnaire-based Methods. Questionnaires are widely used in the field of UX evaluation (Bargas-Avila and Hornbæk, 2011). The *Product Attachment Scale* (Mugge et al., 2006), for example, represents a questionnaire-based evaluation tool to measure the hedonic emotional bonding of a user to a product. On the contrary, *AttrakDiff* (Hassenzahl et al., 2003) analyzes hedonic and pragmatic product attributes via semantic differentials. The summative visualization then again makes it difficult to deduce concrete plans for action in interdisciplinary development projects. For a holistic QUX approach we want to ensure the communication of objective UX goals by incorporating a concrete set of UX characteristics as well as a formative visualization of UX measurements into a visual tool.

3   Methodology

The main goal of this paper is to create a tool that helps interdisciplinary development teams to measure, visualize, and communicate a product's UX. We, therefore, aim to reduce the gap between academia and industrial practice by following a systematic methodological approach (see Figure 1).

Figure 1. Three-phase methodological approach.

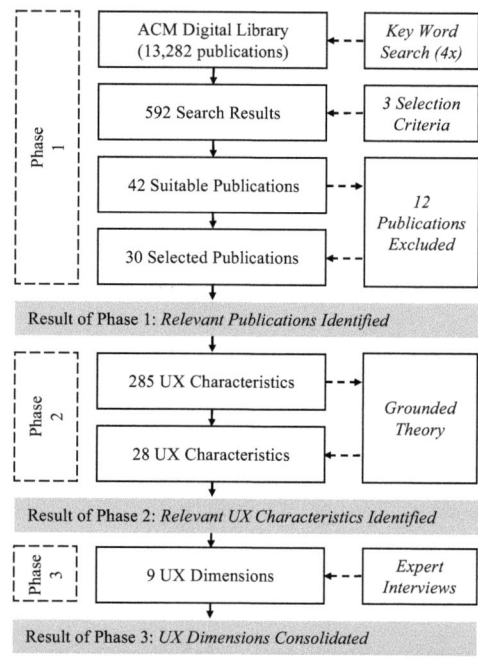

To start with, we pursue an elaboration of UX characteristics based on the analysis of published work in the field of UX. This literature analysis represents a two-phase process with the goal of identifying relevant published work and extracting prevailing UX characteristics that serve as a basis for discussion in the third phase. The third phase of our analysis process consists of expert interviews with practitioners and researchers in the field of UX. Based on that approach, we were able to review a diverse spectrum of UX perspectives and consolidate the extracted characteristics into nine substantial components of UX, which we refer to as "UX dimensions". All in all, the literature analysis does not claim collective exhaustiveness of all possibly existing UX specifications but represents an elaborate foundation to support the subsequent interview process in phase 3.

3.1   Phase 1: Relevant Publications Identified

Source selection. We conducted a selective literature analysis inspired by the methodology of (Bargas-Avila and Hornbæk, 2011) with the ACM Digital Library (DL) as a research database in order to develop a guideline for our expert interviews (phase 3). Within the ACM DL, we selected five conferences and one journal for our source research: The Conference on Human Factors in Computing Systems (CHI), the Conference on Computer Supported Cooperative Work (CSCW), the Symposium on User Interface Software and Technology (UIST), Human Computer Interaction with Mobile Devices and Services (MobileHCI), Transactions on Computer-Human Interaction (TOCHI), and the International Joint Conference on Pervasive and Ubiquitous Computing (UbiComp).

We identified the mentioned venues as sources for top HCI publications based on the h5-index indicated by Google Scholar, and the relevance for the underlying research question. Besides the top three mentions CHI, CSCW, and UIST on Google Scholar we integrated UbiComp and MobileHCI in our analysis as they focus on HCI topics that we considered highly relevant for our research (i.e., mobile/handheld devices). Furthermore, TOCHI complements insights from conference proceedings with findings from an established HCI journal.

Search procedure. We used a set of four combinations for every venue using the ACM DL input mask. The first combination consisted of the key words "user experience" (all of this text) plus "communicate, measure, measuring, visualize, framework, tool, guideline, emotions, usability, evaluate, evaluating, evaluation, satisfaction" (any of this text). The second combination consisted of the key words "measure, emotions" (all of this text), the third of "measure, usability" (all of this text), and the fourth of "user, satisfaction" (all of this text) plus "measure, framework, visualize" (any of this text). The combinations were used to search the publications' abstract in order to focus on publications that are highly relevant for the underlying research question. Furthermore, the particular combinations allowed us to focus on a precise selection of publications to develop a suitable interview guideline for phase 3. We did not limit our search procedure to a specific time span.

Search results. At the time the search was conducted, the ACM DL provided 13,282 publications for the six venues in total. The search process resulted in 592 relevant papers, articles and works-in-progress as illustrated in Table 1.

Table 1. Number of identified publications in phase 1 (by venue).

Venue	Database (ACM DL)	Results per Combination				Selected Publications
		1	2	3	4	
CHI	7,080	192	4	21	70	11
CSCW	3,061	39	3	1	12	2
UIST	1,214	28	0	2	5	1
MobileHCI	991	131	0	6	27	10
TOCHI	518	24	1	5	6	4
UbiComp	418	13	1	0	1	2
SUM	*13,282*		*592*			*30*

Selection process. Before we selected relevant publications from the overall number of search results for phase 2, the authors of this paper (three with an HCI background and two with a business background) jointly defined the following three criteria for a structured selection process: Select publications that *(1)* describe a UX-related framework, such as in Meschtscherjakov et al. (2014), *(2)* analyze UX characteristics of a specific product, such as in Srinivasan et al. (2014), and *(3)* directly discuss UX-related characteristics, such as in Vuolle et al. (2008). However, we excluded 12 publications (e.g., van Schaik et al., 2012) that met one of these criteria but had a focus on UX metrics that have already been covered in our analysis by other identified publications to avoid double results. The se- lection was conducted by the first author, who has extensive knowledge in the field of UX research. Thus, we were able to narrow down the number of relevant publications to 30 (see Table 2).

Table 2. Relevant publications by venue.

Venue	Publications
CHI	Frandsen-Thorlacius et al. (2009), Hart et al. (2013), Hornbæk and Law (2007), Iachello et al. (2006), Kujala et al. (2013), Lee et al. (2015), Meschtscherjakov et al. (2014), Olsson (2014), Olsson and Salo (2012), Rodden et al. (2010), Sonderegger et al. (2014)
CSCW	Cheng (2013), Ju et al. (2008)
UIST	Mueller et al. (2010)
MobileHCI	Jung et al. (2008), Liu et al. (2010), Löchtefeld et al. (2014), Markova et al. (2007), Milic-Frayling et al. (2007), Obrist et al. (2011), Schulze and Kroemker (2012), Turunen et al. (2009), Vandenbroucke et al. (2014), Vuolle et al. (2008)
TOCHI	Hartmann et al. (2008), Karran et al. (2015), Oliveira et al. (2013), Tuch and Hornbæk (2015)
UbiComp	Srinivasan et al. (2014), Vescovi et al. (2014)

3.2   Phase 2: Relevant UX Characteristics Identified

Screening. In this phase, our goal was to detect general UX characteristics within the 30 identified publications. For this purpose, we listed all characteristics that (1) represented UX elements within a theoretical framework, (2) were used to describe a product or service specific UX and (3) were directly mentioned as UX characteristics in any of the 30 publications. In total, we identified 285 UX characteristics.

Consolidation. To reduce the list to a usable number of UX characteristics for our interviews and to derive valuable UX dimensions in phase 3, we followed the interpretive grounded theory research approach by Glaser and Strauss (1971) as well as Isabella (1990). Grounded theory is based on a constant comparison of existing data throughout the analysis process and allows researchers to identify recurring key aspects of qualitative data (Glaser and Strauss, 1971). We were able to recognize seven clusters as well as associated sub-clusters. The outcome of this methodological step is indicated in Table 3. Based on prior experience with the analysis of qualitative UX data, this step was carried on by the first author.

Table 3. Clusters, sub-clusters, and consolidation of identified UX characteristics from the 30 selected publications.

Cluster	Sub-Cluster	*Exemplary characteristics from selected publications*	28 consolidated UX characteristics
Emotions	-	e.g., fun, pleasure producing, happiness, ...	Satisfaction, Pleasure
Design	Form General	e.g., color, clear, interface quality, ... e.g., natural, design, visual appearance, ...	Interface, Aesthetics
Content	Information General	e.g., information quality, information accessed, ... e.g., effectiveness, usefulness, ...	Information, Effectiveness
Technology	Productivity Controllability Progression	e.g., efficiency, efficiency of use, ... e.g., data security, control, safety, ... e.g., easy to learn, usability problems, ...	Efficiency, Functionality, Ease of Use, Performance Usability, Utility, Security, Control, Learnability
Result	Outcome Expectation	e.g., task success, quality, product success, ... e.g., completeness, low error frequency, ...	Quality of Outcome, Error-free
Further Disciplines	Business User Social	e.g., money, brand, communication process, ... e.g., personalization, personification, ... e.g., social context, popularity, recommend, ...	Brand History, Advertisement, Price, Expectation, Customization, Self-realization, Group Affiliation, Social Connectivity
Environment	Temporal Context	e.g., time, memorability, use frequency, ... e.g., device context, implicit interaction, ...	Memorability, Time Context, Location Context

Some authors used rather general *emotions*, such as fun or satisfaction (see Hart et al., 2013; Hornbæk and Law, 2007) as UX characteristics. Further clusters were based on *design-related*, e.g., color or aesthetics (see Hart et al., 2013; Meschtscherjakov et al., 2014), *content-related*, e.g., information quality (see Sonderegger et al., 2014), *technology-related*, e.g., controllable (see Frandsen-Thorlacius et al., 2009), or *outcome-related* characteristics, e.g., error-free (see Turunen et al., 2009). With the clusters *further disciplines* and *environment* we were able to evaluate UX characteristics such as status, brand, or context of use (see Hartmann et al., 2008; Obrist et al., 2011; Vandenbroucke et al., 2014).

Exclusion. We iteratively compared the clusters to narrow down the number of UX characteristics. To ensure a structured analysis process we jointly defined the following exclusion criteria: Exclude UX characteristics that *(1)* are specific for a particular product, such as network speed (see Liu et al., 2010), *(2)* overlap with other UX characteristics, such as social connectivity and social recommendation (see Frandsen-Thorlacius et al., 2009; Olsson and Salo, 2012), and *(3)* are similarly used, such as efficiency of use and efficiency (see Hartmann et al., 2008; Oliveira et al., 2013; Markova et al., 2007). Thus, we ended up with a list of 28 UX characteristics, with all identified clusters represented in our shortlist (see Table 3). However, we realized that these characteristics had not yet offered a clear comprehension of an interdisciplinary QUX approach. To gain a better understanding about practically oriented UX dimensions for interdisciplinary design processes, we used this shortlist as a basis for the interviews in phase 3.

3.3   Phase 3: UX Dimensions Consolidated

Participants. Over the course of one week, we conducted expert interviews with 11 UX researchers and 13 UX practitioners to reflect their respective views. The listing below provides an overview of affiliations (less than 24 values due to companies who asked not to be mentioned). With regard to expert status, all our academic interviewees are (or were) researchers at institutes with a significant track record of publications at leading HCI conferences. As for practice, our sample reflects the perspectives of UX professionals from established firms as well as from emerging, digital startups in the fields of e.g. education, sports, finance, or smart home.

- *University Affiliations:* Aalborg University, University of Bristol, University of Lugano, New Jersey Institute of Technology, University of Oulu (2x), Queensland University of Technology (2x), University of Stuttgart, Tampere University of Technology (2x).

- *Industry Affiliations:* AirBnB, Allianz, GoCardless, Google, IICM, Nokia, Number26, Stylight, Tado, Talentry, Twitter.

Procedure. The first part of our interviews consisted of open questions about disciplines and departments involved in the product development process. In the second part, our experts were presented with our shortlist of the 28 UX characteristics and respective definitions. Participants were asked to complete this table by indicating the most relevant characteristics, reviewing our definitions, and linking them to responsible disciplines. On the basis of the interviews, we were able to narrow our list down to 9 relevant UX dimensions.

4   Results

Below, we structure our findings into two interrelated sections. First, we propose a formalism to quantify UX based on our literature analysis and interviews. Second, we develop a corresponding tool to visualize QUX and to enhance communications within interdisciplinary teams.

4.1   Quantifying UX (QUX)

We analyzed our expert interviews using a qualitative content analysis as proposed by Mayring (2014), with a high inter-rater agreement (Cohen's Kappa $\kappa = .84$; see Cohen, 1960). To start with, we presented our participants with a list of 28 UX characteristics and asked them to select the 10 they regarded as most important. This procedure allowed us to reduce the number of relevant characteristics to 15, which are reported in Table 4. Next, to add more structure and balance, we decided to cluster our dimensions into the categories of *Look*, *Feel*, and *Usability* similar to Norman (2013).

Table 4. Top 5 UX characteristics per category.

Look	*n*
Aesthetics / Design	14
Interface	7
Brand History / Brand Name	5
Information Value	5
Advertisement / Brand	3
Feel	***n***
Control	13
Ease of Use	13
Learnability	12
Pleasure	12
Satisfaction	12
Usability	***n***
Efficiency	11
Utility	11
Effectiveness	10
Functionality	9
System Performance	8

Based on recommendations by our interviewed experts, we then merged some dimensions that were close to each other and/or partly overlapping. This way, we ended up with a total of nine relevant UX dimensions (three per category) as reported in Table 5. In a last step, we developed three corresponding items/questions per dimension (based on existing, pre-tested scales from Bruner et al. (2012), who provide multi-item measures for consumer insight research) to quantify a product's UX via answers on 7-point Likert scales.

Table 5. Interdisciplinary UX dimensions with corresponding questionnaire items and related work for in-depth, follow-up analyses.

Area	Dimension	Scales	ID	Related Work
Look	*Appealing Visual Design*	How balanced and harmonic do you find the product? Do you like the design, colors, fonts used in this product? Do you find the text:image ratio appropriate?	*d1*	Cooper et al. (2014), Hartmann et al. (2008), Lavie and Tractinsky (2004), Sonderegger et al. (2014)
	Communicated Information Structure	Does the product provide clear navigation and orientation? How consistently is the content and information organized? Do you find the provided information understandable?	*d2*	
	Visual Branding	Do you trust this brand? Do you think this is an honest brand? Do you feel the brand is safe?	*d3*	
Feel	*Mastery*	Do you find this product easy to use? Do you find it easy to learn (and remember) how to use the product? Do you feel you have full control over the product?	*d4*	Jordan (1998), Kujala et al. (2011), Kujala and Miron-Shatz (2013), Norman (2013)
	Outcome Satisfaction	How satisfied are you with the outcome? To what extent are you feeling successful with the outcome? How happy are you with the outcome?	*d5*	
	Emotional Attachment	How pleasurable do you find using the product? Does the process of using the product provide you with gratification? Do you feel excited when you are using the product?	*d6*	
Usability	*Task Effectiveness*	Do you think the product does what it is supposed to do? Do you find the product effective? Does the product help you fulfill your task?	*d7*	Hornbæk and Law (2007), Jordan (1998), Nielsen, 1994), Sauro and Lewis (2009)
	Task Efficiency	Is the product the fastest way to achieve your goal? Is the product the most convenient way to achieve your goal? Does using the product fit with your schedule?	*d8*	
	Stability and Performance	Are errors handled well? Does the system run smoothly? Does the product work fast and responsively?	*d9*	

4.2   Visualizing and Communicating QUX

In addition, we asked all interview participants which disciplines should be involved in UX design processes. We identified the most relevant disciplines for each dimension using inductive category formation (see Mayring, 2014). Besides HCI-related disciplines, such as Backend Development or Interaction Design, practitioners and researchers alike considered further disciplines, such as Marketing and Product Management, as highly relevant for the UX design process.

Table 6. Top 10 disciplines involved in the UX design process, sorted by number of occurrence in expert interviews (multiple responses possible).

Top 10 disciplines involved in UX design process	n	Percentage
Backend Development	20	83%
Visual/Graphics Design	18	75%
Marketing	18	75%
Interaction Design	12	50%
Product Management	12	50%
User Research	10	42%
Usability Engineering/Testing	5	21%
UI/Frontend Development	5	21%
General Management	5	21%
Public Relations	3	13%

Table 6 provides an overview of the top ten disciplines involved in the UX design process according to our interviewees. Furthermore, we asked all participants to link the respective disciplines to our list of 28 UX characteristics. Thus, we were able to assign responsibilities (i.e., disciplines) to our nine consolidated UX dimensions (see Figure 1).

Figure 1. Quantified UX evaluation tool (radar diagram represents exemplary outcome for one industry partner after implementation).

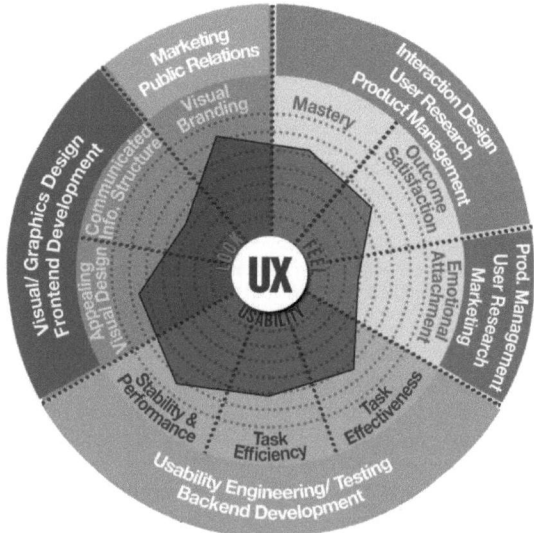

Next, we were interested in practices and tools currently used to communicate goals and objectives in UX design processes. The majority of participants named meetings as the most important forum for discussing UX goals. Specific tools or visualizations are rarely used, whereas prototypes often serve as a basis to illustrate specific UX objectives. However, several UX practitioners described a kind of uncertainty when it comes to communicating UX within teams.

In sum, we were able to derive the following needs for our QUX approach from our interviews: *(1)* Combine measurement scales with a suitable visualization to enhance communication of concrete UX goals, *(2)* realize an easy-to-use application to support practitioners with different levels of expertise, and *(3)* consider the perspectives of different stakeholders as UX is multidisciplinary by nature. These needs are consistent with the findings of Väänänen-Vainio-Mattila et al. (2008a).

Based on our identified needs we developed a graphical tool to measure, visualize, and communicate UX goals within interdisciplinary teams. The visual foundation of our QUX tool is a radar diagram with the categories *Look*, *Feel*, and *Usability* as focus areas. Next, we included the nine UX dimensions as well as the associated disciplines in accordance with the respective category.

The outer circle of the radar diagram connects our dimensions with the respective disciplines and illustrates the need for an interdisciplinary exchange. We designed our tool following a goal-oriented approach (see Hassenzahl, 2008). The UX-related disciplines are therefore centered around the nine UX dimensions (i.e., the UX goals) which represent the core of QUX.

As a final step, the 7-point Likert scale that is used to evaluate a product's UX based on the nine UX dimensions is illustrated as dotted circles. We use the questionnaire as indicated in Table 5 to quantify a product's UX and calculate average scores for each dimension (based on the associated scale). To illustrate a product's quantified UX, the scores for every dimension (be it as mean, median, or confidence interval) can be inserted in the radar diagram, linked, and visualized as a spanned plane (see Figure 1). Thus, development teams can easily detect weak spots in a product's UX and communicate further required actions, from product management over usability engineering to marketing. The basic idea of this visualization is similar to the UX wheel (see Revang, 2007).

5   Evaluation

The goal of our evaluation is to judge the practical applicability of QUX within organizations. This is why we integrated our tool in the design processes of our industry partners and asked for their feedback. We chose to work with partners in the fields of sports, event ticketing, and food delivery to cover a certain range of B2C consumer applications in fast growing industries that increasingly focus on mobile apps. To bring the tool to life (i.e., to discuss with professionals over real QUX scores rather than theoretical ideas), we asked our partners to collect exemplary survey data from their users via a Google form containing our 27 questions.

5.1   Sample Description

Our partner firms collected one large sample (n = 616, by providing a lottery of high-end workout equipment as an incentive) and two smaller samples (n = 18 and n = 21, with no further incentive). Table 7 summarizes the demographic data. For all three samples, we computed Cronbach's α for each UX dimension. As shown in Table 8, alpha values range from .74 to .96, indicating consistently high construct reliabilities (Cronbach, 1951). This indicates that each three items/questions we developed from Bruner et al. (2012) seem to reliably measure the respective UX dimension derived from our methodology. We see this as a promising foundation for subsequent user-driven scale development and empirical studies, as discussed below in our section on future work.

Table 7. Demographic data.

	Sports	Ticketing	Delivery
n	616	18	21
Gender	(m) 24% (f) 76%	(m) 67% (f) 33%	(m) 67% (f) 33%
Age Range	9-56 yrs	n/a	n/a
Average	29 yrs	n/a	n/a

Table 8. Cronbach's α by sample and dimension.

UX Dimension	Sports	Ticketing	Delivery
d1	.87	.95	.75
d2	.89	.95	.81
d3	.90	.95	.92
d4	.88	.96	.86
d5	.91	.89	.93
d6	.93	.95	.86
d7	.88	.93	.85
d8	.84	.94	.92
d9	.88	.95	.74

5.2 Exemplary QUX Analysis

We analyzed the data retrieved from survey respondents and visualized it using our QUX tool. Figure 1 shows an exemplary outcome for an application, which suffers from a rather poorly communicated information structure (users have problems with understanding the product's navigation and structure) and a lack of emotional attachment (users do not identify with the product, do not have any positive memories about the last use, etc.). Beyond this first diagnosis, our tool offers subsequent suggestions which departments or disciplines should be involved when conducting further in-depth UX evaluation. In this case, the *Visual/Graphics* department or *Frontend Developer* could initiate additional A/B-Testing to work towards a better information structure. Furthermore, *Product Management* might meet with *Marketing* to think about ways to improve emotional attachment of users (e.g., include animations or information that motivates recurring usage).

5.3 Qualitative Feedback from UX Professionals

We presented our findings at our partner companies to those responsible for UX (#1: a CTO, #2: a Vice President of Product and Design, and #3: a Senior Product Manager). Across all companies, our QUX tool received consistently positive feedback which falls into the following three categories.

Provides Overview and Helps to Prioritize

All our partners emphasized that the QUX tool provides a good starting point for thinking about UX: *"The tool provides a useful overview of different aspects of UX. I must admit that I haven't had all of them on my radar yet."* (#2) Furthermore, it *"helps to identify strengths and weaknesses, which in turn helps us to prioritize our next steps in development."* (#1) While the high-level overview was greatly appreciated, one product manager added that *"it would be really helpful if you could provide us with some additional, qualitative tools to analyze our weak spots in more detail."* (#3)

Allows for Benchmarking

Another key property of QUX seems to be its suitability for benchmarking: *"For us, it would be highly interesting to conduct the same kind of analysis with our competitors' products to understand where we stand relative to them."* (#3) One of the partners can even imagine *"using the tool to track user experience over time, so that we can track progress in our product development efforts."* (#1) To better judge the significance of the results, he proposed that in a revised version of QUX, we should also think about visualizing standard deviations/variances for each dimension.

Facilitates Communication in Teams

Our partners also emphasized the benefits of our visualization: *"The radar diagram is a smart way of illustration. It helps to bring across the most relevant aspects at first glance. This visualization of UX provides a solid basis for deriving concrete actions."* (#3) Another partner expressed that he finds it helpful because he doesn't *"have to waste time and resources to prepare and visualize the data. So, it really makes sense to agree on one single method, and stick to it."* (#2)

6   Limitations, Future Work, and Conclusion

We see our approach as a first step towards achieving a more common view of UX within and beyond organizations. However, a unified measurement approach comes at the cost of potentially neglecting highly specific product details. While we acknowledge that every product is unique, we are convinced that QUX can be an important first step to obtain an overview and common understanding of a product's UX. In this regard, QUX can be thought of as representing a manual for a toolbox rather than a tool itself. In future work, it might prove useful to not only link QUX findings to the associated disciplines, but to also use them for suggesting evaluation tools and methods for further in-depth analyses.

In our expert interviews, we learned once more that product development processes and respective UX paradigms are still dramatically different from one company to another. Yet, we believe that our approach can be valuable in similarly different ways. For example, early-stage startups might share a much more holistic view on their product and UX, but lack structured processes. Here, QUX can provide a meaningful guideline. With companies increasing in size and industry sectors maturing, the need for departmentalization and number of involved stakeholders is rising steadily. Here, QUX can facilitate efficient communications. To showcase how QUX works in practice, we integrated it into the product development process of firms from three different industries. We found it encouraging that we received positive feedback across industry sectors. Still, a much broader sample drawn from a variety of products, services and sectors might hold many exciting insights. Our primary goal was to design a tool for measuring UX which is both building on and intended for industrial practice. This is why we deducted UX dimensions from expert interviews and then designed and qualitatively evaluated a tool by integrating it into the workflows of our industry partners.

We acknowledge that an alternative approach would have been a user-driven scale development through factor analysis-based dimensional reduction of large-scale surveys (as in, e.g., Bargas-Avila and Hornbæk, 2011). Our work aims at deriving needs from UX experts and practitioners, which we see as a foundation for corresponding empirical work that focuses on the end-user side. Overall, we see QUX as complementary to the landscape of existing UX evaluation methods and as a solid foundation for future work towards a common organizational understanding of UX.

References

Alves, R., Valente, P., & Nunes, N. J. (2014). The State of User Experience Evaluation Practice the State of User Experience Evaluation Practice. In *Proceedings of the 8th Nordic Conference on Human-Computer Interaction (NordiCHI '14)* (pp. 93–102). ACM.

Bakker, S., Markopoulos, P., & de Kort, Y. (2008). OPOS: An Observation Scheme for Evaluating Head-Up Play. In *Proceedings of the 5th Nordic Conference on Human-Computer interaction (NordiCHI '08)* (pp. 18–22). ACM.

Bargas-Avila, J. A., & Hornbæk, K. (2011). Old Wine in New Bottles or Novel Challenges? A Critical Analysis of Empirical Studies of User Experience. In *Proceedings of the SIGCHI Conference on Human Factors in Computing Systems (CHI '11)* (pp. 2689–2698). ACM.

Battarbee, K., & Koskinen, I. (2005). Co-experience: user experience as interaction. *CoDesign, 1*(1), 5–18.

Bruner, G. C., Hensel, P. J., & James, K. E. (2012). *Marketing Scales Handbook: A compilation of multi-item measures for consumer behavior & advertising research.* (6th ed.). American Marketing Association.

Burmester, M., Mast, M., Jäger, K., & Homans, H. (2010). Valence Method for Formative Evaluation of User Experience. In *Proceedings of the 8th ACM Conference on Designing Interactive Systems (DIS '10)* (pp. 364–367). ACM.

Cheng, S. (2013). "Third Eye": Designing Eye Gaze Visualizations for Online Shopping Social Recommendations. In *Proceedings of the ACM 2013 conference on Computer Supported Cooperative Work Companion (CSCW '13)* (pp. 125–128). ACM.

Cohen, J. (1960). A coefficient of agreement for nominal scales. *Educational and Psychological Measurement.*

Cooper, A., Reimann, R., Cronin, D., & Noessel, C. (2014). *About Face. The Essentials of Interaction Design* (4th edition). John Wiley & Sons.

Cronbach, L. (1951). Coefficient alpha and the internal structure of tests. *Psychometrika.* Springer.

Den Uyl, M. J., & van Kuilenburg, H. (2005). The FaceReader: Online facial expression recognition. In *Measuring Behavior 2005, 5th International Conference on Methods and Techniques in Behavioral Research* (pp. 589–590). ACM.

Desmet, P. (2004). Measuring Emotion: Development and Application of an Instrument to Measure Emotional Responses to Products. In *Human-Computer Interaction Series Volume 3. Funology: From Usability to Enjoyment* (pp. 111–123). Kluwer Academic.

Frandsen-Thorlacius, O., Hornbæk, K., Hertzum, M., & Clemmensen, T. (2009). Non-Universal Usability? A Survey of How Usability is Understood by Chinese and Danish Users. In *Proceedings of CHI 2009* (pp. 41–50). ACM.

Glaser, B. G., & Strauss, A. L. (1971). *The Discovery of Grounded Theory: Strategies for Qualitative Research. American Sociological Review* (Vol. 36). Aldine Transaction.

Gray, C. M. (2014). Evolution of Design Competence in UX Practice. In *Proceedings of the SIGCHI Conference on Human Factors in Computing Systems (CHI '14)* (pp. 1645–1654). ACM.

Hart, J., Sutcliffe, a G., & De Angeli, A. (2013). Love it or Hate it! Interactivity and User Types. In *Proceedings of the SIGCHI Conference on Human Factors in Computing Systems Extended abstracts (CHI '13)* (pp. 2059–2068). ACM.

Hartmann, J., Sutcliffe, A., & Angeli, A. De. (2008). Towards a theory of user judgment of aesthetics and user interface quality. *ACM Transactions on Computer-Human Interaction, 15*(4), 1–30.

Hassenzahl, M. (2008). User experience (UX): Towards an experiential perspective on product quality. In *Proceedings of the 20th International Conference of the Association Francophone d'Interaction Homme-Machine (IHM '08)* (pp. 11–15).

Hassenzahl, M., Burmester, M., & Koller, F. (2003). AttrakDiff: Ein Fragebogen zur Messung wahrgenommener hedonischer und pragmatischer Qualität. In J. Ziegler & G. Szwillus (Eds.), *Mensch & Computer 2003. Interaktion in Bewegung* (pp. 187–196). B.G. Teubner.

Hassenzahl, M., & Tractinsky, N. (2006). User experience - a research agenda. *Behaviour & Information Technology, 25*(2), 91–97.

Helander, M. G., & Zhang, L. (1997). Field studies of comfort and discomfort in sitting. *Ergonomics, 40*(9), 895–915.

Hellman, M., & Rönkkö, K. (2008). Is User Experience Supported Effectively in Existing Software Development Processes? In *Proceedings of the International Workshop on Meaningful Measure: Valid Useful User Experience Measurement (VUUM 2008)* (pp. 32–37).

Hornbæk, K., & Law, E. L.-C. (2007). Meta-Analysis of Correlations Among Usability Measures. In *Proceedings of the SIGCHI Conference on Human Factors in Computing Systems Extended abstracts (CHI '07)* (Vol. 1, pp. 617–626). ACM.

Iachello, G., Truong, K. N., Abowd, G. D., Hayes, G. R., & Stevens, M. (2006). Prototyping and Sampling Experience to Evaluate Ubiquitous Computing Privacy in the Real World. In *Proceedings of the SIGCHI Conference on Human Factors in Computing Systems (CHI '06)* (pp. 1009–1018). ACM.

Isabella, L. A. (1990). Evolving Interpretations as a Change Unfolds: How Managers Construe Key Organizational Events. *Academy of Management Journal, 33*(1), 7–41.

Jordan, P. W. (1998). Human factors for pleasure in product use. *Applied Ergonomics, 29*(1), 25–33.

Ju, W., Lee, B. A., & Klemmer, S. R. (2008). Range: Exploring Implicit Interaction through Electronic Whiteboard Design. In *Proceedings of the ACM 2008 conference on Computer Supported Cooperative Work Companion (CSCW '08)* (pp. 17–26). ACM.

Jung, Y., Anttila, A., & Blom, J. (2008). Designing for the Evolution of Mobile Contacts Application. In *Proceedings of the 10th international conference on Human computer interaction with mobile devices and services (MobileHCI '08)* (pp. 449–452). ACM.

Karapanos, E., Martens, J.-B., & Hassenzahl, M. (2010). On the Retrospective Assessment of Users' Experiences Over Time: Memory or Actuality? In *Proceedings of the SIGCHI Conference Extended Abstracts on Human Factors in Computing Systems (CHI EA '10)* (pp. 4075–4080). ACM.

Karapanos, E., Zimmerman, J., Forlizzi, J., & Martens, J. (2009). User Experience Over Time: An Initial Framework. In *Proceedings of the SIGCHI Conference on Human Factors in Computing Systems (CHI '09)* (pp. 729–738). ACM.

Karran, A. J., Fairclough, S. H., & Gilleade, K. (2015). A Framework for Psychophysiological Classification within a Cultural Heritage Context Using Interest. *ACM Transactions on Computer-Human Interaction, 21*(6).

Kujala, S., & Miron-Shatz, T. (2013). Emotions, experiences and usability in real-life mobile phone use. In *Proceedings of the SIGCHI Conference on Human Factors in Computing Systems (CHI '13)* (pp. 1061–1070). Paris, France: ACM. https://doi.org/10.1145/2470654.2466135

Kujala, S., Roto, V., Väänänen-Vainio-Mattila, K., Karapanos, E., & Sinnelä, A. (2011). UX Curve: A method for evaluating long-term user experience. *Interacting with Computers, 23*(5), 473–483.

Lavie, T., & Tractinsky, N. (2004). Assessing dimensions of perceived visual aesthetics of web sites. *International Journal of Human Computer Studies, 60*(3), 269–298.

Law, E. L.-C., Roto, V., Hassenzahl, M., Vermeeren, A. P. O. S., & Kort, J. (2009). Understanding, scoping and defining user experience. In *Proceedings of the SIGCHI Conference on Human Factors in Computing Systems (CHI '09)* (pp. 719–728). ACM.

Lee, J. M., Jeong, S. Y., & Ju, D. Y. (2015). Emotional Interaction and Notification of Flexible Handheld Devices. In *Proceedings of the SIGCHI Conference Extended Abstracts on Human Factors in Computing Systems (CHI EA '15)* (pp. 2025–2030). ACM.

Liu, N., Liu, Y., & Wang, X. (2010). Data Logging plus E-diary: Towards an Online Evaluation Approach of Mobile Service Field Trial. In *Proceedings of the 12th international conference on Human computer interaction with mobile devices and services (MobileHCI '10)* (pp. 287–290). ACM.

Löchtefeld, M., Lautemann, N., Gehring, S., & Krüger, A. (2014). ambiPad – Enriching Mobile Digital Media with Ambient Feedback. In *Proceedings of the 16th international conference on Human-computer interaction with mobile devices & services (MobileHCI '14)* (pp. 295–298). ACM.

Markova, M., Aula, A., Vainio, T., Wigelius, H., & Kulju, M. (2007). MoBiS-Q: a tool for evaluating the success of mobile business services. In *Proceedings of the International Conference on Human Computer Interaction with Mobile Devices and Services (MobileHCI '07)* (pp. 238–245). ACM.

Mayring, P. (2014). *Qualitative Content Analysis: Theoretical Foundation, Basic Procedures and Software Solution.*

Meschtscherjakov, A., Wilfinger, D., & Tscheligi, M. (2014). Mobile Attachment - Causes and Consequences for Emotional Bonding with Mobile Phones. In *Proceedings of the SIGCHI Conference on Human Factors in Computing Systems (CHI '14)* (pp. 2317–2326). ACM.

Milic-Frayling, N., Hicks, M., Jones, R., & Costello, J. (2007). On the Design and Evaluation of Web Augmented Mobile Applications. In *Proceedings of the 9th international conference on Human computer interaction with mobile devices and services (MobileHCI '07)* (pp. 226–233). ACM.

Mueller, F. "Floyd," Vetere, F., Gibbs, M., Edge, D., Agamanolis, S., & Sheridan, J. (2010). Jogging over a Distance between Europe and Australia. In *Proceedings of the 23nd annual ACM symposium on User interface software and technology (UIST '14)* (pp. 189–198). ACM.

Mugge, R., Schifferstein, H. N. J., & Schoormans, J. P. L. (2006). A Longitudinal Study of Product Attachment and its Determinants. *European Advances in Consumer Research, 7,* 641–647.

Nielsen, J. (1994). Enhancing the Explanatory Power of Usability Heuristics. In *Conference Companion on Human Factors in Computing Systems (CHI '94)* (pp. 152–158). ACM.

Norman, D. A. (2013). *The Design of Everyday Things.* Basic Books.

Obrist, M., Beck, E., Wurhofer, D., & Tscheligi, M. (2011). Experience Characters: A Design Tool for Communicating Mobile Phone Experiences to Designers. In *Proceedings of the International Conference on Human Computer Interaction with Mobile Devices and Services (MobileHCI '11)* (pp. 385–394). ACM.

Oliveira, R. De, Cherubini, M., & Oliver, N. (2013). Influence of Personality on Satisfaction with Mobile Phone Services. *ACM Transactions on Computer-Human Interaction, 20*(2), 1–23.

Olsson, T. (2014). Layers of User Expectations of Future Technologies: An Early Framework. In *Proceedings of the SIGCHI Conference Extended Abstracts on Human Factors in Computing Systems (CHI EA '14)* (pp. 1957–1962). ACM.

Olsson, T., & Salo, M. (2012). Narratives of satisfying and unsatisfying experiences of current mobile augmented reality applications. In *Proceedings of the SIGCHI Conference on Human Factors in Computing Systems Extended abstracts (CHI '12)* (p. 2779). ACM.

Pine, J., & Gilmore, J. H. (1998). Welcome to the Experience Economy. *Harvard Business Review, 76*(4), 97–105.

Revang, M. (2007). User Experience Project: The User Experience Wheel. Retrieved September 12, 2017, from http://userexperienceproject.blogspot.de/2007/04/user-experience-wheel.html.

Rodden, K., Hutchinson, H., & Fu, X. (2010). Measuring the User Experience on a Large Scale : User-Centered Metrics for Web Applications. In *Proceedings of the SIGCHI Conference on Human Factors in Computing Systems (CHI '10)* (pp. 2395–2398). ACM.

Roto, V., Lee, M., Pihkala, K., Castro, B., Vermeeren, A., Law, E., Obrist, M. (2015). All About UX. Information for user experience professionals. Retrieved September 12, 2017, from http://www.allaboutux.org/.

Sauro, J., & Lewis, J. R. (2009). Correlations among Prototypical Usability Metrics: Evidence for the Construct of Usability. In *Proceedings of the SIGCHI Conference on Human Factors in Computing Systems (CHI '09)* (pp. 1609–1618). ACM.

Schulze, K., & Kroemker, H. (2012). Extracting User Experience Centered Product Requirements for Mobile Social Media Applications. In *Proceedings of the 14th international conference on Human-computer interaction with mobile devices and services companion (MobileHCI '12)* (pp. 143–148). ACM.

Scollon, C. N., Kim-Prieto, C., & Diener, E. (2003). Experience Sampling: Promises and Pitfalls, Strengths and Weaknesses. *Journal of Happiness Studies, 4*(1), 5–34.

Sheldon, K. M., Elliot, A. J., Kim, Y., & Kasser, T. (2001). What Is Satisfying About Satisfying Events? Testing 10 Candidate Psychological Needs. *Journal of Personality and Social Psychology, 80*(2), 325–339.

Sonderegger, A., Uebelbacher, A., Pugliese, M., & Sauer, J. (2014). The influence of aesthetics in usability testing. In *Proceedings of the SIGCHI Conference on Human Factors in Computing Systems (CHI '14)* (pp. 21–30). ACM.

Srinivasan, V., Moghaddam, S., Mukherji, A., Rachuri, K. K., Xu, C., & Tapia, E. M. (2014). MobileMiner: Mining Your Frequent Patterns on Your Phone. In *Proceedings of the 2014 ACM International Joint Conference on Pervasive and Ubiquitous Computing (UbiComp '14)* (pp. 389–400). ACM.

Tuch, A. N., & Hornbæk, K. (2015). Does Herzberg's Notion of Hygienes and Motivators Apply to User Experience? *ACM Transactions on Computer-Human Interaction, 22*(4).

Turunen, M., Melto, A., Hella, J., Heimonen, T., Hakulinen, J., Mäkinen, E., Soronen, H. (2009). User Expectations and User Experience with Different Modalities in a Mobile Phone Controlled Home Entertainment System. In *Proceedings of the International Conference on Human Computer Interaction with Mobile Devices and Services (MobileHCI '09)* (pp. 1–4). ACM.

Väänänen-Vainio-Mattila, K., Roto, V., & Hassenzahl, M. (2008a). Now Let's Do It in Practice: User Experience Evaluation Methods in Product Development. In *Proceedings of the SIGCHI Conference on Human Factors in Computing Systems Extended abstracts (CHI '08)* (pp. 3961–3964). ACM.

Väänänen-Vainio-Mattila, K., Roto, V., & Hassenzahl, M. (2008b). Towards Practical User Experience Evaluation Methods. In *Proceedings of the International Workshop on Meaningful Measure: Valid Useful User Experience Measurement (VUUM 2008)* (pp. 19–22). Institute of Research in Informatics of Toulouse (IRIT).

van Schaik, P., Hassenzahl, M., & Ling, J. (2012). User-Experience from an Inference Perspective. *ACM Transactions on Computer-Human Interaction, 19*(2), 1–25.

Vandenbroucke, K., Ferreira, D., Goncalves, J., Kostakos, V., & De Moor, K. (2014). Mobile Cloud Storage: A Contextual Experience. In *Proceedings of the International Conference on Human Computer Interaction with Mobile Devices and Services (MobileHCI '14)* (pp. 101–110). ACM.

Vermeeren, A. P. O. S., Law, E. L.-C., Roto, V., Obrist, M., Hoonhout, J., & Väänänen-Vainio-Mattila, K. (2010). User experience evaluation methods: current state and development needs. In *Proceedings of the 6th Nordic Conference on Human-Computer Interaction (NordiCHI '10)* (pp. 521–530). ACM.

Vescovi, M., Bruno, L., Perentis, C., Moiso, C., & Leonardi, C. (2014). My Data Store: Toward User Awareness and Control on Personal Data. In *Proceedings of the 2014 ACM International Joint Conference on Pervasive and Ubiquitous Computing (UbiComp '14)* (pp. 179–182). ACM.

Vuolle, M., Tiainen, M., Kallio, T., Vainio, T., Kulju, M., & Wigelius, H. (2008). Developing a Questionnaire for Measuring Mobile Business Service Experience. In *Proceedings of the 10th international conference on Human computer interaction with mobile devices and services (MobileHCI '08)* (pp. 53–62). ACM.

IV   Article 3

The Effects of Visual Control Mechanisms on Touch-based Mobile Devices[1]

Abstract

A major limitation for selling physical products via the Internet appeared to be the lack of information obtained by the sense of touch. However, the rapid adoption of touch-based mobile devices has increased the possibilities to provide multisensory product experiences online. The focus of our work is to investigate the interaction effects between digital touchscreen interfaces and visual control mechanisms on consumer choice and willingness to pay. We explore the effects of the most frequently used visual control mechanisms, *zoom technology* and *alternative photo technology*, in two experimental studies. First, we test our hypotheses in a field experiment comprising of 467,132 observations in 193,255 unique sessions where we observe consumers' product interest and product purchase decisions. Second, we conduct an online experiment on mobile devices with 804 subjects to understand the underlying psychological mechanisms and to explore the moderating role of textural fit between a touchscreen and the surfaces of different products. Our results contribute to the understanding of virtual product experience in computer-mediated environments in multiple ways. First, we contribute to the literature of visual control mechanisms. The findings from both experiments indicate that alternative photo technology leads to decreased product interest but higher willingness to pay, while zoom technology has no similar effects. Second, we show that these effects of visual control mechanisms are substantially different on touch-based mobile devices compared to PC interfaces: positive interaction effects between alternative photos technology and touch indicate increased product interest. Third, we establish textural fit as an important driver of object valuation on touch devices.

Keywords: *mobile, consumer touch, visual control, sensory marketing, product choice*

---

[1] This article is based on the following working paper: Naegelein, P. & Spann, M. (2017). *The Effects of Visual Control Mechanisms on Touch-based Mobile Devices*. Working Paper. LMU Munich.

1   Introduction

A major limitation for selling physical products via the Internet appeared to be the lack of information obtained by the sense of touch (Peck and Childers, 2003a; 2003b). Therefore, it was theorized that non-touch shopping in (electronic) non-touch media may never be able to replace traditional retail shopping, in particular for products which differ in material properties. Hence, researchers and practitioners alike have been exploring ways how to compensate for touch (Peck et al., 2013). In this regard, Mooy and Robben (2002) describe product experience on a continuum from direct (e.g., holding a product in one's hands) to indirect (e.g., reading an advertisement or written product description). The more direct and interactive the experience, the more senses are involved.

In the past decade, we have not only witnessed the emergence of a variety of technologies that allow for enriched multimedia, but also the rapid adoption of touch-based devices such as smartphones and tablet PCs. Thus, possibilities to enhance product experience through multisensory interaction, e.g., by combining touch and vision, have increased significantly (Streicher and Estes, 2016). Interdisciplinary literature on information systems, sensory marketing and consumer psychology offers insights into the process of how individuals evaluate and interact with products in the digital world. Specifically, we focus on the interplay between visual control mechanisms and touch-based mobile devices.

Visual control mechanisms. When shopping online, consumer interaction with the product is usually restrained to computer-mediated, indirect experiences. To address this challenge, retailers increasingly rely on innovative presentation formats to reduce frictions and enable virtual product inspection (Li et al., 2002). Visual control mechanisms comprise all web technologies which enable customizable presentation formats and ways of navigation (Jiang and Benbasat, 2005). Frequently used technologies offered in online shops include, for instance, *zoom* and *alternative photo* technology (e.g., De et al., 2013). Web shops offering zoom technology enable their customers to enlarge product photos and view details, such as fabric, more closely. Alternative photo technology provides users with multiple product pictures from different angles, oftentimes in context (e.g., a model wearing a piece of clothing). One step further, *360-degree product spin* technology provides higher degrees of object control and resembles direct touch in brick-and-mortar retail store even more closely (e.g., Verhagen et al., 2014). Lastly, *augmented reality* technology enables virtual mirror presentation formats. The cameras built into computers and mobile devices let users integrate virtual objects into real-world environments so that they can assess how, e.g., a couch would fit into their personal living room (Verhagen et al., 2014). In summary, visual control mechanisms enable multisensory product experiences and increase consumer engagement (Blazquez Cano et al., 2016).

Touch-based mobile devices. The literature stream about the effect of computer-mediated touch interfaces on consumer behavior is still in its infancy (Shen et al., 2016; Peck et al., 2013). Related research has mainly been conducted in the fields of human-computer interaction and multichannel shopping. For instance, Xu et al. (2017) examine the capabilities of tablet computers relative to PCs and smartphones. They find that the tablet channel mostly complements the smartphone channel, while it substitutes the PC channel. Prior studies highlight device-specific differences in screen size, portability, and resulting user behavior (e.g., Ghose et al., 2013; Kim et al., 2011; Wang et al., 2015). Within the context of consumer behavior, focus has recently shifted to the capabilities of touchscreen interfaces, which most mobile devices bring along (cf. DeviceAtlas, 2016).

A key question for the ability of touch-based interfaces to create multi-sensory experiences is whether evaluating objects through digital touch can resemble physically touching the actual product. Schlosser (2003) shows that the perceived touchability of haptic products stimulates mental simulation and increases ownership feelings, especially when haptic characteristics are diagnostic (Grohmann et al., 2007). Peck and Shu (2009) demonstrate that merely touching an object can be sufficient to create perceived ownership. Such feelings of possession can be increased using direct touch interfaces (compared to using touchpads and computer mice) since the nature of interaction resembles direct physical touch more closely (Brasel and Gips, 2014). This analogy is moderated by interface ownership, driven by perceived control and associations of touch devices as the consumer's extended self. Furthermore, Shen et al. (2016) illustrate how touchscreen interfaces enhance mental product interaction, facilitating the choice of affect-laden products such as hedonic food.

A closely related but different literature stream investigates the role of functional control mechanisms, which determines how humans interact with objects through computer mediated interfaces. The two axial dimensions of functional control (vividness and object interactivity; established by Steuer, 1992) can enhance online product presentations and increase consumers attitudes and intentions (Jiang and Benbasat, 2007). Roggeveen et al. (2015), for instance, find that dynamic presentation formats such as video portrayals increase consumer involvement, willingness to pay, and preference for hedonically superior products.

The focus of our work, in contrast to previous research, is to investigate the interaction effects between visual control mechanisms and digital touchscreen interfaces, as online shopping is rapidly shifting from electronic to mobile commerce. First, we explore the effects of the most frequently used visual control mechanisms, *zoom* and *alternative photo* technology, on consumer choice in their online purchasing process. To investigate the differential effects of these two visual control mechanisms, we provide empirical data from a field experiment comprising of 467,132 observations in 193,255 unique sessions along two stages of the buying process, product interest and product purchase. Second, and most importantly, we are interested in the moderating role of touchscreen interfaces. Our experimental setup allows us to single out customers using touch-based mobile devices, such as smartphones and tablets, and to explore their interaction effects with zoom and alternative photo technology. Third, we conduct an additional online experiment on mobile devices with 804 subjects to gain further insights into how the relationship between visual control mechanisms and consumers' willingness to pay is influenced by the degree of textural fit between a touchscreen and the surfaces of different products.

The remainder of this study is organized as follows. We first derive our hypotheses from theory on visual control, human-computer interaction and consumer psychology. Next, we describe the design, sample, and results of our field experiment. Then, we outline the setting and results of our online experiment. To conclude, we provide a general discussion of the results from the two experiments and derive managerial implications as well as directions for further research.

2 Theory and Methodology

In the following, we outline the research model of this study (see Figure 1), derive our hypotheses, and explain our methodology.

Figure 1. Research Model.

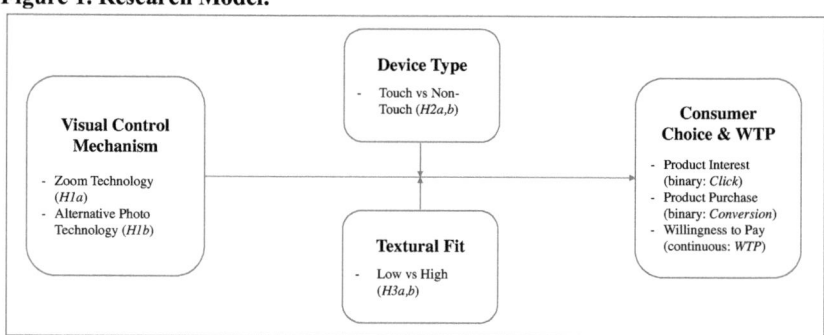

2.1 The Effect of Visual Control Mechanisms on Product Interest and Purchase

Computer-mediated interfaces used in online shopping create a barrier to touch (Peck and Childers, 2003). Laroche et al. (2005) compare traditional brick-and-mortar stores with online shopping and demonstrate the consequences of intangibility on evaluation difficulty and perceived risk, since the lack of experiential product information online creates uncertainty among consumers about subjective quality (Dimoka et al., 2012; Wood, 2001). To mitigate such information loss, many online retailers have adopted zoom and/or alternative photo technology.

Thus, we argue that the relationship between visual control mechanisms and consumer decisions is driven by type and quality of the product information obtained through digital interaction. In this regard, Holbrook (1978) distinguishes between *factualness* and *evaluativeness* as key dimensions of content communication.

Zoom technology and factual information. Factual information is defined as "logical, objectively verifiable descriptions of tangible product features" (Holbrook, 1978; p. 547). Hence, we expect that presentation formats increasing the factualness of product information should reduce the risk and uncertainty of buying online since content is perceived as more credible. Zoom technology, for instance, allows online shoppers to look at product details more closely. This way, consumers can extract additional factual information about product details such as fabric, workmanship or ornaments.

Alternative photo technology and evaluative information. Evaluative information can be described as "subjective impressions of intangible aspects of the product" (Holbrook, 1978; p. 547). This may correspond to alternative product photos, which provide contextual information helping consumers form individual opinions. While the first image usually depicts the focal products surrounded by a white background, additional pictures oftentimes display how the product is used – e.g., how a model is wearing a handbag or how furniture fits into a living room. In addition, multiple photos might also provide factual information when showing the product from different angles, approximating a three-dimensional rotation (Daugherty et al., 2005). However, De et al. (2013) find that for alternative photo technology, the evaluative information conveyed via contextualization dominates the factual information conveyed via rotation.

Jiang and Benbasat (2005) describe the psychological mechanism underlying both cases as perceived diagnosticity, i.e., "the perceived ability of a Web interface to convey to customers relevant product information that helps them in understanding and evaluating the quality and performance of products sold online" (p. 117). Increased product understanding and diagnosticity result in more positive attitudes toward the website and increased purchase intentions (Jiang and Benbasat, 2007). Jiang and Benbasat (2005) demonstrate that higher levels of visual control (compared to static images) increase perceived diagnosticity for corresponding product attributes. Hence, we expect that both of our visual control mechanisms, zoom and alternative photo technology, increase perceived diagnosticity and lead to increased product interest and product purchase. Therefore:

H1a: *Zoom technology has a <u>positive</u> effect on product interest and product purchase.*

H1b: *Alternative photo technology has a <u>positive</u> effect on product interest and product purchase.*

2.2   The Moderating Effect of Touch Devices

Brasel & Gips (2014) observe a higher degree of perceived ownership and product endowment when products are examined via touch-based mobile devices compared to laptop or desktop PCs that come with trackpads or computer mouse devices. Within this context, interface ownership plays a decisive role, reinforcing the importance of mobile phones as truly personal devices. Smartphones and tablets, in particular when personally owned, seem to be perceived as one's extended self, resulting in more intense relationship bonds with the device (Hein et al., 2011; Wang and Nelson, 2014). Furthermore, direct touch interfaces appear to increase user engagement and bias product evaluations towards tangible attributes (Brasel and Gips, 2015).

Tangibility levels can strongly differ between the offline and online world (e.g., Laroche et al., 2005). Kim and Krishnan (2015) take the example of a dress, which falls in the category of search goods in brick-and-mortar stores, but becomes an experience good in the online world where the opportunity of physical touch and try-on is not available. The search attributes in question can be further classified into *geometric and material attributes* (Klatzky et al., 1993; Lederman and Klatzky, 1990). Klatzky et al. (1990) demonstrate that geometric properties (such as the size or shape of a can of soda) are best explored through the modality of vision, and that material properties (such as texture, weight, or hardness of a piece of clothing) are best explored through the modality of touch. We argue that zoom technology increases factual information to assess geometric properties, whereas alternative photo technology increases evaluative information to assess material properties.

This rationale suggests that the effects of zoom and alternative photo technology should differ between touch devices and non-touch devices. Specifically, we expect that while zoom technology improves visual exploration, smaller screen sizes may complicate product inspection on mobile devices (particularly on smartphones). In contrast, touchscreens should amplify the evaluative information conveyed by alternative photo technology and positively affect consumer decisions, i.e., product interest and product purchase. Thus:

H2a: *Touch devices negatively moderate the relationship between zoom technology and product interest / product purchase.*

H2b: *Touch devices positively moderate the relationship between alternative photo technology and product interest / product purchase.*

2.3   The Moderating Effect of Textural Fit

Any interaction between visual control mechanisms and touch devices leads to the question whether some (material) products are better suited for exploration through visual control mechanisms on touch devices than others. McCabe and Nowlis (2003) demonstrate that customers tend to prefer retailers who allow them to touch their products before purchase, in particular when tactile input is important for quality assessment, e.g., for fashion items or consumer electronics. Grohmann et al. (2007) show that the evaluation of material products is positively affected through tactile input which is diagnostic especially when product quality is high. Schlosser (2003) found that the perceived touchability of products high in haptic importance increase mental simulation and, in turn, psychological ownership. Attractive product design and smooth surfaces trigger hedonic touch, while rough surface textures and increasing shape complexity were shown to be less inviting to touch and feel (Klatzky and Peck, 2012).

These findings are explained by Cognitive Dissonance Theory that predicts unpleasant feelings of dissonance when an experience is inconsistent with previous expectations (Festinger, 1957). Brasel and Gips (2014) transfer this logic to shopping on touch-based mobile devices and showed that touchability moderates the relationship of digital touch and ownership feelings. Applied to touchscreens, the degree of textural dissonance can be described as the difference in perception between the expected product texture of a physical product (e.g., a stone's rough, bumpy surface) and the actual, experienced texture of the digital interface (mostly a smooth, glasslike surface on touchscreens).

Hence, when examining products on touch devices through visual control mechanisms, we expect that consumer decisions will be positively affected by higher levels of textural fit. Conversely, we expect a negative effect for products characterized by a lower degree of textural fit, since the overall interactive experience might feel unfamiliar and lead consumers to delay or stop the purchasing process. Such a line of reasoning implies that the effect of visual control mechanisms on touch devices is amplified by increasing levels of a pleasing interactive experience. Since the concept of textural fit is based on object properties - specifically, the surface - we expect a change in object valuation, through, e.g., consumers' willingness to pay. Therefore:

H3a: *The degree of textural fit positively moderates the relationship between zoom technology and consumers' willingness to pay on touch devices.*

H3b: *The degree of textural fit positively moderates the relationship between alternative photo technology and consumers' willingness to pay on touch devices.*

2.4 Methodology

We test our hypotheses in two experimental studies. First, we conduct a field experiment which provides us with objective data on actual consumer decisions in their purchasing process in the context of an affiliate website and an associated online retailer. Specifically, we can control for device type as well as external factors and observe consumer decisions along two stages of consumer's purchasing process, product interest and product purchase. Second, we conduct an online experiment on mobile phones. This setting allows us to manipulate the degree of textural fit and collect additional insights, in particular about the role of product information and haptic properties, through a follow-up survey. Furthermore, we can complement the binary choice setting of online shops with the measurement of consumers' willingness to pay. This way, we can gain a better understanding of how both visual control mechanisms and textural fit affect object valuation.

3 Field Experiment

In the following, we outline our experimental design, provide model free tests of our hypotheses as well as the results of an econometric analysis.

3.1 Experimental Design and Measures

Our dataset stems from an affiliate shopping website for lifestyle and fashion products, and one of their largest partner shops, a leading European online fashion retailer. Our sample consists of visitors who accessed the affiliate site either via organic search for the affiliate brand or via entering the domain directly into their browser in one large European country. We do not include users from paid traffic which may be biased by the specific ad or by deep links to a specific product. The website itself was fully responsive and thus available on any device equipped with an internet browser. Thus, our experiment ran on touch and non-touch devices alike. When presented with a specific product, participants faced the choice to either click (or tap) on a button redirecting them to the partner shop where the respective item could be purchased (measured as *click*), or to leave the site without any further action. In case of a redirection to the partner shop, our users faced another decision: to buy or not to buy the product selected (measured as *conversion*).

Experimental manipulation. In our field experiment, we experimentally manipulated the way products were presented to prospective buyers. More precisely, we altered the visual control mechanisms available to explore the respective fashion item. We used a 2x2 between-subjects experimental design with random assignment of participants to experimental groups. As first experimental factor, we either enabled zoom technology to allow for obtaining factual information through product details such as fabric, or not. As second experimental factor, we either enabled alternative photo technology to allow for the gathering of evaluative information through additional pictures, or not.

Hence, each participant was randomly assigned to one of the following four treatment groups when starting a session: "zoom disabled, alternative photos disabled" (group 1, our control group, which resembles the affiliate site's usual design); "zoom enabled, alternative photos disabled" (group 2); "zoom disabled, alternative photos enabled" (group 3); and "zoom enabled, alternative photos enabled" (group 4, as depicted in Figure 2). Over the course of eight days, the website operator agreed to randomly assign all users who had landed on their homepage (via organic search and direct traffic) to one of our four experimental groups. The underlying randomization process was performed by a server-sided allocation mechanism so that participants had no ability to self-select into a treatment group. Users remained within the same experimental group throughout their respective session. Based on the visits of users in 193,255 unique sessions, the dataset consists of 467,132 page impressions (i.e., observations) in total (which are fairly evenly split into our four treatment groups: group 1: 113,786 impressions, group 2: 113,358 impressions, group 3: 117,777 impressions, group 4: 122,211 impressions). In total, 164,852 different products were displayed. In our dataset, a user session consists of 2.4 product impressions on average, with the same product viewed 1.1 times on average within the same session.

Figure 2. Field Experiment: Product Presentation (*Left*: Smartphone View, Zoom Enabled and Alternative Photos Enabled; *Center*: Exemplary Product View Using Zoom Technology; Right: Exemplary Product View Using Alternative Photo Technology).

 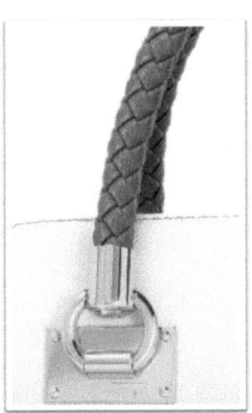 

Measures. Our focal variables are *click* (users choosing to proceed to the partner shop) and *conversion* (users choosing to buy the respective product at the partner shop). Device-specific effects can be accounted for through categorization of devices, based on their browser and viewport[2], into touch (smartphone and tablet) and non-touch devices (desktop and laptop). Time-specific effects are covered by the time of the day (i.e., morning, afternoon, evening, night), and the day of the week. Product-specific control variables include the product category (female, male, or unisex/unspecified) and the product's price.

In summary, our dataset covers session-level information on all user activities along the purchasing process. We can accurately observe which products are viewed when and on which device type, whether a consumer chooses to be redirected to the partner shop, and whether a final purchase was made. Please note that the data are anonymous and do not contain any type of personal information.

---

[2] The term *viewport* stems from responsive web design and can be described as the area of a web page visible to the user. It varies with device type and is and typically reported as portrait x landscape width, e.g., 375x667 pixels for an iPhone 6.

Table 1. Field Experiment: Summary Statistics.

Variable	No. of Obs.	Mean	Std. Dev.	Min	Max
Impressions per Session	193,255	2.416	3.781	1	224
Impressions per Session and Product	193,255	1.081	.457	1	56
Click (DV)	467,132	.089	.285	0	1
Conversion (DV)	467,132	.008	.091	0	1
Smartphone (DV)	467,132	.395	.489	0	1
Tablet (DV)	467,132	.217	.412	0	1
Desktop (DV)	467,132	.388	.487	0	1
Monday (DV)	467,132	.112	.315	0	1
Tuesday (DV)	467,132	.192	.394	0	1
Wednesday (DV)	467,132	.226	.418	0	1
Thursday (DV)	467,132	.115	.319	0	1
Friday (DV)	467,132	.108	.310	0	1
Saturday (DV)	467,132	.115	.319	0	1
Sunday (DV)	467,132	.132	.339	0	1
Night (00:00 - 05:59 am / DV)	467,132	.038	.191	0	1
Morning (06:00 - 11:59 am / DV)	467,132	.201	.401	0	1
Afternoon (12:00 - 05:59 pm / DV)	467,132	.366	.482	0	1
Evening (06:00 - 11:59 pm / DV)	467,132	.395	.489	0	1
Impression of Female Product (DV)	467,132	.751	.432	0	1
Impression of Male Product (DV)	467,132	.243	.429	0	1
Impression of Unisex Product (DV)	467,132	.003	.051	0	1
Product Price (in €)	41,621	102.92	85.86	4.75	2669.95

Notes: 467,132 page impressions; 193,255 user sessions, 41,621 conversions. DV: Dummy variable.

3.2   Test of Hypotheses: Model Free Results

Figure 3 shows the average click-through and conversion rates for our four experimental treatment groups. In our control group (group 1), we measure a click-through rate (CTR) of 10.9 percent and a conversion rate (CR) of 9.1 percent. In comparison, we observe a small but significant difference in group 2 (with zoom technology enabled), with CTR down to 10.4 percent (Δ = -.4 percent; $p < .01$) and CTR down to 8.4 percent (Δ = -.7 percent; $p < 0.1$). These gaps widen in group 3 (with alternative photo technology enabled): relative to our control group, CTR falls to 7.1 percent (Δ = -3.8 percent; $p < .01$) while CR rises to 10.2 percent (Δ = +1.1 percent; $p < .01$).

We see similar results in group 4 (characterized by the availability of zoom and alternative photos), with CTR down to 7.2 percent (Δ = -3.7 percent; $p < .01$) and CR up to 10.1 percent (Δ = +1.0 percent; $p < .01$). All pairwise differences of group means are significant, except for group 3 and 4 (see Tables 2a and 2b for further details).

Figure 3. Field experiment: average click-through and conversion rates (compared to control group).

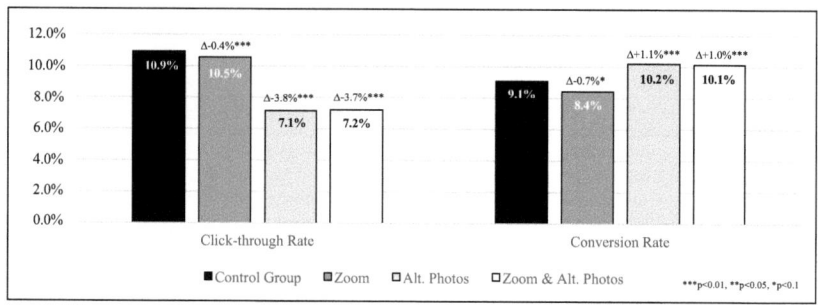

Table 2a. Field experiment: model free results for click.

Group (I)	Group (J)	Mean Diff. (I-J)	Sig.		Std. Err.	95% Confidence Interval	
Group 1 (No Zoom; No Alt. Photos)	Group 2	.004	.005	***	.001	.001	.006
(Mean: .109)	Group 3	.038	.000	***	.001	.035	.040
	Group 4	.036	.000	***	.001	.034	.039
Group 2 (Zoom; No Alt. Photos)	Group 1	- .004	.005	***	.001	- .006	- .001
(Mean: .105)	Group 3	.034	.000	***	.001	.032	.036
	Group 4	.033	.000	***	.001	.031	.035
Group 3 (No Zoom; Alt. Photos)	Group 1	- .038	.000	***	.001	- .040	- .035
(Mean: .071)	Group 2	- .034	.000	***	.001	- .036	- .032
	Group 4	- .001	.221		.001	- .003	.001
Group 4 (Zoom; Alt. Photos)	Group 1	- .036	.000	***	.001	- .039	- .034
(Mean: .072)	Group 2	- .033	.000	***	.001	- .035	- .031
	Group 3	.001	.221		.001	- .001	.003

*No. of Obs.: 467,132. Two-sample t-tests with equal variances. *** p<.01, ** p<.05, * p<.10*

Table 2b. Field experiment: model free results for conversion.

Group (I)	Group (J)	Mean Diff. (I-J)	Sig.		Std. Err.	95% Confidence Interval	
Group 1 (No Zoom; No Alt. Photos)	Group 2	.006	.079	*	.004	- .001	.013
(Mean: .091)	Group 3	- .011	.006	***	.004	- .020	- .003
	Group 4	- .011	.008	***	.004	- .019	- .003
Group 1 (Zoom; No Alt. Photos)	Group 1	- .006	.079	*	.004	- .013	.001
(Mean: .084)	Group 3	- .018	.000	***	.004	- .026	- .010
	Group 4	- .017	.000	***	.004	- .025	- .009
Group 3 (No Zoom; Alt. Photos)	Group 1	.011	.006	***	.004	.003	.020
(Mean: .102)	Group 2	.018	.000	***	.004	.010	.026
	Group 4	.001	.896		.005	- .008	.010
Group 4 (Zoom; Alt. Photos)	Group 1	.011	.008	***	.004	.003	.019
(Mean: .101)	Group 2	.017	.000	***	.004	.009	.025
	Group 3	- .001	.896		.005	- .010	.008

No. of Obs.: 41,621. Two-sample t-tests with equal variances. *** p<.01, ** p<.05, * p<.10

Figure 4 illustrates click-through and conversion rates clustered by device type. Most notably, we observe that - across all treatment groups - product interest and purchase are higher on non-touch devices, with a CTR of 11.2 percent and a CR of 10.2 percent. Interestingly, we find both click-through (CTR of 7.5 percent; $\Delta = -3.7$ percent; $p < .01$) and conversion (CR of 6.5 percent; $\Delta = -3.7$ percent; $p < .01$) to be substantially lower when users were shopping on touch devices.

Figure 4. Field experiment: average click-through and conversion rates for touch and non-touch devices.

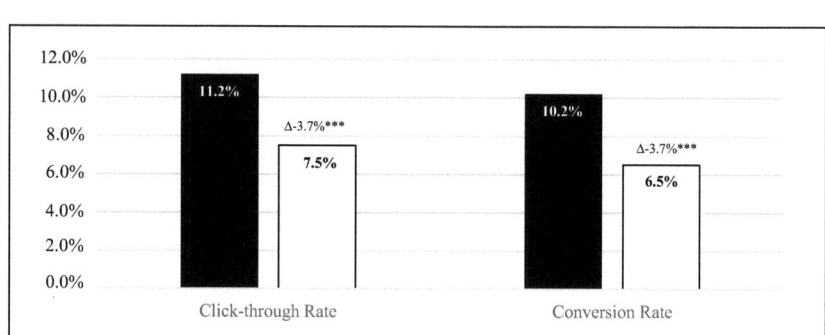

3.3   Test of Hypotheses: Econometric Models
The aim of the econometric analysis is to look more closely at the role of device types to understand whether certain effects of visual control mechanisms can be attributed to specific interfaces.

Model and coding. Our data allows us to analyze consumer decisions along two stages, *click* and *conversion.* Our 467,132 observations are clustered into 193,255 unique user sessions, which is why we need to account for session-level randomization. In the first stage, we model consumer choice probability as a function of session-specific, product-specific, and time-specific variables. Our conversion data in the second stage is dependent on the first stage – i.e., we can only observe consumers who chose to be forwarded to the partner shop (41,462 observations in 22,621 unique sessions). Therefore, we estimate both stages using a Heckman sample selection model to correct for self-selection (Heckman, 1979). Following the model specification as proposed by Cameron and Trivedi (2010), conversion, our second and final stage, is modeled as binary choice equation:

(1)   prob (CONVERSION = 1) =
Φ ($\beta_{ijt} + \beta_1$ * ZOOM$_{ijt} + \beta_2$ * PHOTOS$_{ijt} + \beta_3$ * ZOOM$_{ijt}$ * PHOTOS$_{ijt}$ + β_4 * TOUCHDEVICE$_{ijt}$ + β_5 * TOUCHDEVICE$_{ijt}$ * ZOOM$_{ijt}$ + β_6 * TOUCHDEVICE$_{ijt}$ * PHOTOS$_{ijt}$ + β_7 * TOUCHDEVICE$_{ijt}$ * ZOOM$_{ijt}$ * PHOTOS$_{ijt} + \beta_8$ * PRICE$_{ijt}$ + ε_{2ijt})
= Φ ($Z_{2ijt}\beta$)

where $\Phi(\cdot)$ denotes the standard normal cumulative distribution function, subscripts i denote page impression, j denote session, and t denote time. Our selection equation corresponds to all observations where conversion is observed:

(2)   prob (CLICK = 1) =

Φ (γ_{ijt} + γ_1 * ZOOM$_{ijt}$ + γ_2 * PHOTOS$_{ijt}$ + γ_3 * ZOOM$_{ijt}$ * PHOTOS$_{ijt}$ + γ_4 * TOUCHDEVICE$_{ijt}$ + γ_5 * TOUCHDEVICE$_{ijt}$ * ZOOM$_{ijt}$ + γ_6 * TOUCH-DEVICE$_{ijt}$ * PHOTOS$_{ijt}$ + γ_7 * TOUCHDEVICE$_{ijt}$ * ZOOM$_{ijt}$ * PHOTOS$_{ijt}$ + γ_8 * FEMALE$_{ijt}$ + γ_9 * WEEKEND$_{ijt}$ + γ_{10} * MORNING$_{ijt}$ + γ_{11} * AFTERNOON$_{ijt}$ + γ_{12} * EVENING$_{ijt}$ + ε_{1ijt})

= Φ ($\mathbf{Z_{1ijt}}\gamma$) > 0

Our model assumes that error terms follow a normal distribution and are independent of both sets of explanatory variables:

(3)   (ε_{1ijt}, ε_{2ijt}) ~ N (0, 0, $\sigma^2_{\varepsilon_{1ijt}}$, $\sigma^2_{\varepsilon_{2ijt}}$, $\rho_{\varepsilon_{1ijt}\varepsilon_{2ijt}}$)

(4)   (ε_{1ijt}, ε_{2ijt}) independent of $\mathbf{Z_{1ijt}}$ and $\mathbf{Z_{2ijt}}$

Based on a maximum likelihood estimator, we jointly estimate our two stages in a Heckman model:

(5)   prob (CONVERSION|Z_2, CLICK = 1) = Φ ($\mathbf{Z_{2ijt}}\beta$) + $\rho\sigma_{\varepsilon_{1ijt}\varepsilon_{2ijt}}\lambda$ ($\mathbf{Z_{1ijt}}\gamma$)

where ρ denotes the correlation between unobserved determinants of click and conversion (ε_{1ijt}, ε_{2ijt}), $\sigma_{\varepsilon_{1ijt}\varepsilon_{2ijt}}$ represents the standard deviation of (ε_{1ijt}, ε_{2ijt}), and λ measures the inverse Mills ratio at click stage. To reflect the dummy variables defining our treatment groups (zoom and alternative photos) and their interaction, we chose an effect-coding approach. Specifically, we assigned a dummy value of -0.5 if the respective technology was disabled, and + 0.5 if the respective technology was enabled.

Results. Our results (see Table 3) show that the estimated coefficient ρ indicates a significant negative correlation between error terms in both the full model (ρ = -.116; $p < .01$) and reduced model (ρ = -.116; $p < .01$). Furthermore, the Wald tests of independent equations for the full model (ρ = 0: $\chi^2(1)$ = 35.17; $Prob. > \chi^2$ = .000) and reduced model (ρ = 0: $\chi^2(1)$ = 34.83; $Prob. > \chi^2$ = .000) point at significant correlation, suggesting that the Heckman selection model is appropriate for further analysis. Our full model reveals that the type of visual control mechanism significantly impacts consumer decisions across devices. While providing the opportunity to obtain factual information through zoom technology seems to have no effect (γ_1 = -.025; $p > .10$ for *click*), we see major, significant effects when enabling alternative photo technology and provide evaluative product information (γ_2 = -.282; $p < .01$ for *click*). We measure slightly different effects in our reduced model (i.e., excluding interaction effects). Zoom technology becomes slightly significant at click stage (γ_1 = -.018; $p < .10$) and alternative photo technology becomes significant at conversion stage (β_2 = .021; $p < .01$). When combining zoom and alternative photo technology, the two effects seem to partially offset each other, resulting in the most favorable outcome along the funnel (γ_3 = .065; $p < .01$ for *click*). Thus, Hypothesis 1a and 1b must be rejected.

The effects of visual control mechanisms vary between devices in direction and strength. Across treatment groups, we observe negative effects for touch devices such as smartphones and tablets (γ_4 = -.269; $p < .01$ for *click* and β_4 = -.021; $p < .01$ for *conversion*) compared to our baseline, non-touch devices. However, the interactions terms reveal significant moderation effects of touch devices: while providing zoom technology has no effect on click rates when using touch devices (γ_5 = -.005; $p > .10$ for *click*), alternative photo technology leads to positive effects on touch devices (γ_6 = .086; $p < .01$ for *click*). Hence, only Hypothesis 2b is supported. Our control variables yield expected effects: choice probability is higher for female products (γ_8 = .271; $p < .01$ for *click*). There is a higher likelihood of product interest on weekends (γ_9 = .099; $p < .01$ for *click*) compared to weekdays, as well as in the morning (γ_{10} = .073; $p < .01$ for *click*), afternoon (γ_{11} = .077; $p < .01$ for *click*), and evening (γ_{12} = .067; $p < .01$ for *click*) compared to night hours. Lastly, the likelihood of a product purchase slightly decreases with higher product prices (β_{11} = -2.51e^{-06}; $p < .10$ for *conversion*). We find consistent results in our reduced model.

Table 3. Field experiment: Heckman selection model (clustered by session).

VARIABLES	Full Model		Reduced Model	
	Click	Conversion	Click	Conversion
Zoom (DV[a])	-0.025	-0.018*	-0.008	-0.004
	[0.021]	[0.009]	[0.010]	[0.005]
Alternative Photos (DV[b])	-0.282***	0.012	-0.219***	0.021***
	[0.021]	[0.010]	[0.010]	[0.005]
Zoom x Alt. Photos	0.065**	0.020		
	[0.031]	[0.015]		
Touch Device (DV[c])	-0.269***	-0.021**	-0.242***	-0.011**
	[0.020]	[0.008]	[0.010]	[0.005]
Touch Device x Zoom	0.005	0.024*		
	[0.028]	[0.014]		
Touch Device x Alt. Photos	0.086***	0.012		
	[0.027]	[0.014]		
Touch Device x Zoom x Alt. Photos	-0.064	-0.031		
	[0.041]	[0.021]		
Product Type: Female (DV[d])	0.271***		0.271***	
	[0.012]		[0.012]	
Weekend (DV[e])	0.099***		0.099***	
	[0.011]		[0.011]	
Morning (06.00 am - 11.59 am) (DV[f])	0.072**		0.071**	
	[0.029]		[0.029]	
Afternoon (12.00 pm - 05:59 pm) (DV[f])	0.076***		0.075***	
	[0.028]		[0.028]	
Evening (06.00 pm - 11:59 pm) (DV[f])	0.067**		0.066**	
	[0.028]		[0.028]	
Product Price		$-2.51e^{-06}$*		$-1.78e^{-06}$*
		[0.000]		[0.000]
Constant	-1.383***	0.165***	-1.404***	0.158***
	[0.032]	[0.012]	[0.030]	[0.011]
Observations	467,132	41,621	467,132	41,621
Unique Sessions	193,255	22,689	193,255	22,689
Rho		-0.116		-0.115
Sigma		0.292		0.292
Lambda		-0.034		-0.033
atrho		-0.116 [0.020] ***		-0.115 [0.020] ***
lnsigma		-1.230 [0.013] ***		-1.230 [0.013] ***

Standard errors in brackets

*** p<.01, ** p<.05, *p<.10

DV: Dummy variable. Baseline a: no zoom b: no alternative photos c: non-touch device,

d: male or unspecified product, e: weekday, f: night (00.00 am - 05.59 am)

3.4   Discussion of the Field Experiment

First, it becomes apparent that visual control mechanisms can have a significant impact on the purchasing process. More precisely, our results show that different types of visual control technologies lead to opposite effects. Zoom technology, conveying factual information alone, does not seem to influence the purchasing process, neither at click nor at conversion stage. This could be explained by the phenomenon that only a fraction of customers makes use of the opportunity to zoom into product details. In contrast, we observe significant effects for alternative photo technology. Contrary to our hypotheses, however, consumer decisions were impacted in a negative way: many users abandoned the purchasing process at the click stage. Our model-free results indicate that this phenomenon is partially countered by higher conversion rates, pointing at information front-loading: among those who continued to the partner shop, the conversion rate was higher compared to our control group. Interestingly, combining zoom and alternative photo technology yields the most favorable results in our econometric model: factual and evaluative information seem to complement each other. Taken together, our findings indicate that visual control mechanisms alter the decision-making process along our two stages of click and conversion.

Second, we observe significant effects for touch-based mobile devices. Click and conversion rates are substantially lower compared to desktop PCs – a finding consistent with previous research and industry experience. While providing zoom technology does not seem to make any difference, alternative photo technology shows positive interaction effects. The effect is particularly noteworthy, especially when compared with the overall negative effect of alternative photo technology: this visual control mechanism leads to opposite results on touch devices compared to non-touch devices. We attribute this observation to the evaluative information about material properties, amplified by the modality of touch.

4   Online Experiment

In the following, we outline our experimental design and provide model-free tests of our hypotheses as well as an econometric analysis.

4.1   Experimental Design and Measures

In our online experiment, we replicate the two experimental dimensions of our field experiment (zoom and alternative photo technology) and add a third one: textural fit. Our sample consists of 804 respondents on Amazon Mechanical Turk (AMT) who completed the whole task on their smartphones. Participants were presented with an online shopping scenario and asked to form an opinion about the respective product. Thereafter, they answered a set of questions via an online survey displayed on the same device.

Pretest. The goal of our product-side manipulation in the online experiment was to induce a variation in textural fit between the surfaces of a smartphone touchscreen and of the objects to be evaluated. In a pretest, we asked 34 university students to rate perceived textural fit (Gerlach and Buxmann, 2011) of different pairs of products on a three-item Likert-type scale. Travel mugs emerged as suitable pair, with similar geometric, but varying material properties. More precisely, we chose one mug made of porcelain (a rather smooth and glass-like surface, inducing a higher textural fit of $\mu = 2.39$), and one made of cork (a rather rough surface, inducing lower textural fit of $\mu = 1.54$), with a mean difference significant at $p < .01$.

Figure 5. Online experiment: product presentation (*left*: porcelain mug for high textural fit; *right*: cork mug for low textural fit).

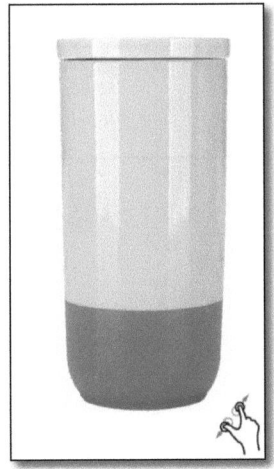

Experimental manipulation. Our experiment is characterized by a 2 (*textural fit:* low vs. high) x 2 (*zoom technology*: disabled vs. enabled) x 2 (*alternative photo technology*: disabled vs. enabled) design, with the three factors manipulated between subjects. Overall, our sample consists of eight distinct treatment groups (see Figure 5 for examples).

Measures. In our online experiment, we measure consumers' willingness to pay (WTP, reported in USD) as key dependent variable. This way, we can obtain additional insights into how visual control mechanisms influence consumer decisions, since price points in our field experiment had been fixed by the retailers. Furthermore, our experimental setting allows us to analyze the underlying psychological mechanisms. Via seven-point Likert-type scales, we measure perceived information control (based on the perceived diagnosticity scale by Jiang and Benbasat, 2005; and the behavioral control scale by Dabholkar, 1996; van Dolen et al., 2007) as well as perceived ownership (Pierce et al. 2001; Pierce et al. 2003). Furthermore, we measured the following control variables: need for touch (both autotelic and instrumental, Peck and Childers, 2003a), age, gender, and familiarity with smartphone shopping to account for specific consumer characteristics (see appendix for measurement scales). Summary statistics are provided in Table 4.

Table 4. Online experiment: summary statistics.

Variable	Mean	Std. Dev.	Min	Max
Zoom (DV)	0	0,5	-0,5	0,5
Alternative Photos (DV)	-0,01	0,5	-0,5	0,5
Textural Fit (DV)	0	0,5	-0,5	0,5
WTP (in USD)	10,88	6,24	0	50
Haptic Experience	2,98	1,4	1	7
Perceived Ownership	3	1,84	1	7
Perceived Information Control	4,65	1,44	1	7
Autotelic NFT	5,25	1,33	1	7
Instrumental NFT	5,52	1,25	1	7
Female	0,47	0,5	0	1
Age	33,37	9,01	18	71
Familiarity	5,89	1,4	1	7

No. of obs.: 804 subjects. DV: Dummy variable.

4.2   Test of Hypotheses: Model Free Results

Manipulation Check. A two-sample t-test with equal variances suggests that the desired manipulation of textural fit was successful. We found perceived textural fit, reported on a three-item seven-point Likert-type scale (Cronbach's α = .76), to be significantly higher ($p < .05$) for the porcelain mug (n = 407, μ = 3.08, 95% CI [2.93; 3.22]) compared to the cork mug (n = 397, μ = 2.89, 95% CI [2.76; 3.02]).

Willingness to Pay. As illustrated in Figure 6, we observe significantly higher WTP amounts in the high textural fit (i.e., porcelain mug) condition (n = 407, μ = 12.41, 95% CI [11.77; 13.05]) than in the low textural fit (i.e., cork mug) condition (n = 397, μ = 9.31, 95% CI [8.78; 9.86]) across all presentation formats ($p < .01$). Within the low textural fit condition, the availability of visual control mechanisms does lead to different values of WTP compared to our control group (no zoom and no alternative photos), however at insignificant levels ($p > .10$). Interestingly, we see different results in the high textural fit condition. Relative to our control group (μ = 10.73), we observe significantly higher WTP when zoom technology is enabled (μ = 12.62, Δ = 1.89, $p < .01$), alternative photo technology is enabled (μ = 13.12, Δ = 2.39, $p < .01$), or both (μ = 13.51, Δ = 2.78, $p < .01$). Hence, Hypotheses 3a and 3b are supported.

Figure 6. Online Experiment: Average Willingness to Pay for High and Low Textural Fit, Compared to Control Group.

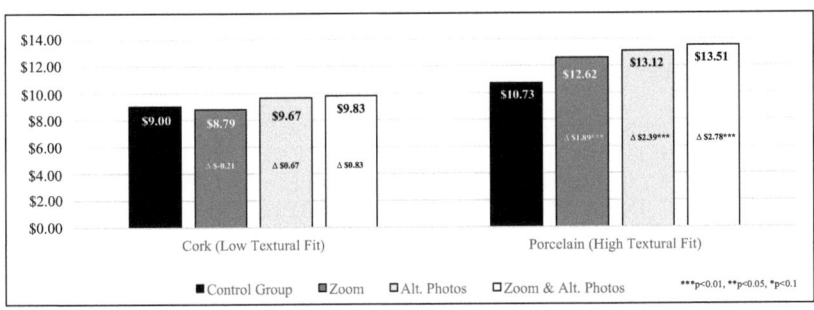

Perceived Information Control. Another goal of our online experiment was to gain more insights into the psychological mechanisms to explain the superior performance of alternative photo technology compared to zoom technology. While we did not find any significant differences between our treatment groups for the *perceived ownership* construct (Cronbach's α = .97), our *perceived information control* construct (Cronbach's α = .88) reveals substantial differences (see Figure 7). On the one hand, zoom functionality has no significant effects on perceived information control (μ = 4.55, Δ = -.17, $p > .10$ for low textural fit; μ = 4.34, Δ = -.17, $p > 0.10$ for high textural fit) compared to our control group. On the other hand, we see a significant difference for alternative photos relative to our control group (μ = 5.27, Δ = +.55, $p < .01$ for low textural fit; μ = 4.54, Δ = +.37, $p < .01$ for high textural fit). Note that perceived information control seems to be consistently higher in the low textural fit condition (total mean difference across treatment groups of $\Delta = +.51, p < .01$). Formal mediation analysis (Preacher and Hayes 2004; 2008) reveals a significant indirect effect ($b = -.24, p < .05$) of perceived information control between textural fit and WTP. For our remaining two independent variables (zoom and alternative photos), however, we do not find significant mediation effects.

Figure 7. Online experiment: average perceived information control for high and low textural fit, compared to control group.

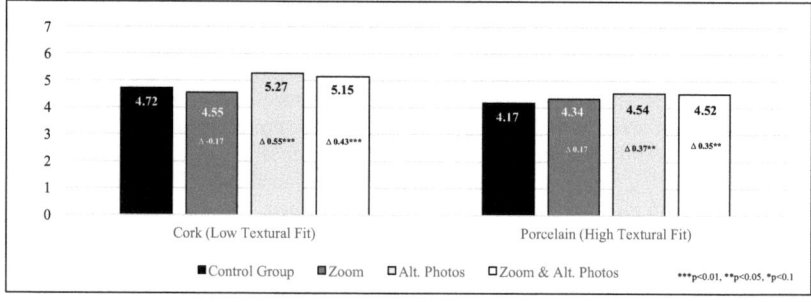

4.3   Test of Hypotheses: Econometric Analysis

Regression model and coding. We use an OLS regression model with consumers' willingness to pay (in USD) as dependent variable:

(2) $WTP_i = \alpha + \beta_1 * TEXFIT_i + \beta_2 * ZOOM_i + \beta_3 * PHOTOS_i + \beta_4 * ZOOM_i * PHOTOS_i + \beta_5 TEXFIT_i * ZOOM_i + \beta_6 * TEXFIT_i * PHOTOS_i + \beta_7 * TEXFIT_i * ZOOM_i * PHOTOS_i + \beta_8 * FEMALE_i + \beta_9 * PERC\_OWN_i + \gamma_{10} * PERC\_INFOCONTROL_i + \beta_{11} * AUTOTELIC\_NFT_i + \beta_{12} * INSTRUMENTAL\_NFT_i + \beta_{13} * FAMILIARITY_i + \beta_{14} * AGE_i + \varepsilon_i$

where subscripts i denotes an individual consumer. Comparable to our field experiment, we use an effect coding approach to reflect the dummy variables defining our treatment groups (zoom, alternative photos, and textural fit) and their interaction. Specifically, we assigned a dummy value of -.5 if the respective technology was disabled (or textural fit was *low*, in the cork mug condition), and + .5 if the respective technology was enabled (or textural fit was *high*, in the cork mug condition).

Table 5. Online experiment: regression model on willingness to pay (WTP).

VARIABLES	WTP	
	Full Model	Reduced Model
Textural Fit (DV[a])	3.334***	3.336***
	[.426]	[.426]
Zoom (DV[b])	.630	.621
	[.418]	[.418]
Alternative Photos (DV[c])	1.119***	1.100**
	[0.427]	[.427]
Zoom x Alternative Photos	-.796	
	[.838]	
Textural Fit x Zoom	.876	
	[.836]	
Textural Fit x Alt. Photos	.959	
	[.838]	
Textural Fit x Zoom x Alt. Photos	-1.576	
	[1.672]	
Female (DV[d])	.829*	.793*
	[.430]	[.429]
Perceived Ownership	.373***	.369***
	[.125]	[.125]
Perceived Information Control	.157	.160
	[.169]	[.168]
Autotelic NFT	.305	.312
	[.193]	[.193]
Instrumental NFT	-.163	-.170
	[.198]	[.197]
Familiarity	.036	.035
	[.156]	[.156]
Age	-.056**	-.057**
	[.023]	[.023]
Constant	9.619***	9.681***
	[1.564]	[1.556]
No. of Obs.	804	804
R-squared	.119	.114

*Standard errors in brackets, *** $p<.01$, ** $p<.05$, * $p<.10$*

DV: Dummy variable. Baseline (=0): [a] low textural fit, [b] no zoom, [c] no alt. photos, [d] male

Results. As shown in Table 5 (left column), our results complement our findings from the field experiment. We now find partial support for Hypothesis 1b, in a sense that visual control through alternative photos technology positively affects consumers' willingness to pay ($\beta_3 = 1.119$; $p < .01$). Zoom technology, in contrast, does not show any significant effects ($\beta_2 = .630$; $p > .10$). Most notably, textural fit has a substantial impact on WTP across treatment groups ($\beta_1 = 3.334$; $p < .01$). We measure, however, no significant effects for interaction terms between each two out of three independent variables ($\beta_4 = -.796$, $\beta_5 = .876$, $\beta_6 = .959$, $\beta_7 = 1.576$; $p > .10$).

While perceived ownership seems to increase WTP ($\beta_9 = .373$; $p < .01$), we do not observe such a direct effect for perceived information control ($\beta_{10} = .157$; $p > .10$), autotelic NFT ($\beta_{11} = .305$; $p > .10$), or instrumental NFT ($\beta_{12} = -.163$; $p > .10$). Further, we find that WTP is higher for women ($\beta_8 = .829$; $p < .10$) and slightly decreasing with age ($\beta_8 = .056$; $p < .05$). All main effects remain significant and of similar magnitude when estimating a reduced model excluding interaction terms (see Table 5, right column).

4.4   Discussion of the Online Experiment

The results of the online experiment are informative in several ways. First, we could replicate the findings of our field experiment and show that not visual control per se, but the specific type of technology affects consumer decisions: the provision of alternative photo technology substantially outperforms zoom technology. We were able to complement our binary choice setting in the field with the continuous measure of willingness to pay and find that our experimental manipulation leads to significantly higher product valuations.

Second, textural fit seems to play a crucial role during the choice process. Not only do we find consistently higher levels of WTP, but textural fit seems to amplify the effects of visual control mechanisms as well. The more pleasant touch experience in the high textural fit condition seems to amplify particularly the effect of alternative photo technology, which fosters the exploration of material properties through the modality of touch.

Third, our insights into perceived information control indicate that evaluative product information (through alternative photo technology) plays a far more important role than factual product information when shopping on smartphones. This effect increases with lower textural fit, which suggest that evaluative information becomes particularly important when uncertainty is high.

5   General Discussion and Conclusion

In this study, we explored the effects of visual control mechanisms on consumer choice and willingness to pay. Using data from two randomized experiments in the field and online laboratory, we further examine the moderating role of touch-based mobile devices and textural fit. Our results contribute to the understanding of virtual product experience in computer-mediated environments in multiple ways.

First, we contribute to the literature of visual control mechanisms. Combined findings from both experiments indicate that zoom and alternative photo technology affect consumers in different ways. These observations indicate that the underlying psychological mechanism is not primarily of affective nature (such as vividness or mental product interaction in the presence of functional control mechanisms, as discussed in, e.g. Roggeveen et al., 2015; Shen et al., 2016), but driven by differences in communicating product information. Our findings are consistent with De et al. (2013), who examined the effects of zoom and alternative photo usage on product returns. Specifically, we add insights into the effects of visual control mechanisms along a two-stage purchasing process and show that alternative photo technology increases product valuation.

Second, our results indicate that the effects of visual control mechanisms on consumer decisions are substantially different on touch-based mobile devices. While technologies conveying evaluative information through the modality of touch positively affect consumer choice and willingness to pay on mobile devices, technologies conveying factual information through the modality of vision can have the opposite (or, no) effect. These findings add to the emerging research stream on exploring products on touch-based mobile devices (e.g., Brasel and Gips, 2014; Brasel and Gips, 2015; Shen et al., 2016).

Third, from a product-related point of view, another contribution of this study is its exploration of textural fit as a key driver of object evaluation on touch devices. Brasel and Gips (2014) distinguish between physical and non-physical products, whereas Shen et al. (2016) focus on hedonic and utilitarian attributes. Building upon this work, we analyze product- and device-related characteristics in a joint examination of surface texture and the resulting haptic experience. This way, we add another dimension to the discussion of whether certain products are more feasible for mobile offerings than others – an increasingly important consideration in the light of increased mobile shopping (e.g., Xu et al., 2017).

Our results hold some more general insights for managerial practice. When designing for interaction, marketers should be aware of the complex interplay between different types of visual control, product-specific characteristics of their offerings, and their customers' primary touch points across device types. For instance, our finding that alternative photo technology negatively impacts click rates on desktop PCs but leads to increased product interest on touch-based mobile devices suggests that there is a potentially underestimated challenge for responsive web design: it might be advantageous to enable certain visual control mechanisms for touch devices only. Furthermore, the results of our field experiment led our industry partner to engage in optimizing the degree of visual control with regard to the contractual agreement with their partner shops: whenever remuneration is based on a cost-per-click basis (i.e., *click*), offering static product images only might be the superior choice. Whenever compensation is based on a cost-per-order basis (i.e., *conversion*), however, providing visual control through multiple product images is likely to be more promising. Lastly, as shown in our online experiment, alternative photo technology increases consumers' willingness to pay – this way of product presentation could thus be of particular relevance in shopping scenarios where pricing power is delegated to consumers, such as in *Name Your Own Price* (NYOP) or *Pay What You Want* (PWYW) offerings (e.g., Krämer et al., 2017).

Our study is subject to some limitations which provide multiple avenues for future research and encourage more granular studies of product evaluation through digital touch. During our field experiment, we were not able to control for multichannel shopping. In light of our finding that visual control mechanisms can have substantially different effects on touch and non-touch devices, it might be valuable to track user interaction in closed shopping ecosystems across platforms. Moreover, our study reveals some indication but no clear evidence explaining why alternative photo technology significantly outperforms zoom technology in both studies. While previous literature and our model-free results hint at perceived information control as driving force, we do not observe respective indirect effects in the online experiment. Future research, examining psychological effects that mediate consumer choice, could explore how information control and textural fit considerations can be, for instance, deliberately integrated into more holistic interactive processes (such as online configurators and customization tools, e.g., Franke et al. 2010) to increase product purchase and valuation.

The control-, interface-, and product-specific factors mentioned above can be molded and recombined to explore a variety of new, interactive experiences that lay the groundwork for augmented and virtual reality applications (Altarteer et al., 2016). This way, senses beyond vision and touch could be gradually involved to mimic interacting with the actual, physical product. Against this background, we believe our findings encourage future studies in the growing and evolving field of sensory marketing and interactive user experiences in a digitized world.

References

Altarteer, S., Vassilis, C., Harrison, D., & Chan, W. (2016). Product Customization: Virtual Reality and New Opportunities for Luxury Brands Online Trading. In *Proceedings of the 21st International Conference on Web3D Technology - Web3D '16* (pp. 173–174). ACM.

Blazquez Cano, M., Perry, P., Ashman, R., & Waite, K. (2017). The influence of image interactivity upon user engagement when using mobile touch screens. *Computers in Human Behavior*, 1–7.

Brasel, S. A., & Gips, J. (2014). Tablets, touchscreens, and touchpads: How varying touch interfaces trigger psychological ownership and endowment. *Journal of Consumer Psychology*, 24(2), 226–233.

Brasel, S. A., & Gips, J. (2015). Interface Psychology: Touchscreens Change Attribute Importance, Decision Criteria, and Behavior in Online Choice. *Cyberpsychology, Behavior, and Social Networking*, 18(9), 534–538.

Cameron, A. C., & Trivedi, P. K. (2010). *Microeconometrics using Stata*. Stata Press.

Dabholkar, P. A. (1996). Consumer evaluations of new technology-based self-service options: An investigation of alternative models of service quality. *International Journal of Research in Marketing*, 13(1), 29–51.

Daugherty, T., Li, H., & Biocca, F. (2005). *Experiential Ecommerce: A Summary of Research Investigating the Impact of Virtual Experience on Consumer Learning*. (C. Haugtvedt, K. Machleit, & R. Yalch, Eds.), *Online Consumer Psychology: Understanding and Influencing Consumer Behavior in the Virtual World*. Lawrence Erlbaum Associates.

De, P., Hu, Y. (Jeffrey), & Rahman, M. S. (2013). Product-Oriented Web Technologies and Product Returns: An Exploratory Study. *Information Systems Research*, 24(4), 998–1010.

DeviceAtlas. (2016). Most popular viewport size statistics for 2016. Retrieved September 16, 2017, from https://deviceatlas.com/blog/viewport-size-statistics-2016.

Dimoka, A., Hong, Y., & Pavlou, P. A. (2012). On Product Uncertainty in Online Markets: Theory and Evidence. *MIS Quarterly*, 36(2), 395–426.

Kim, Y., & Krishnan, R. (2015). On Product-Level Uncertainty and Online Purchase Behavior: An Empirical Analysis. *Management Science*, 61(10), 2449–2467.

Festinger, L. (1957). *A theory of cognitive dissonance*. Stanford University Press.

Franke, N., Schreier, M., & Kaiser, U. (2010). The "I Designed It Myself" Effect in Mass Customization. *Management Science*, 56(1), 125–140.

Gerlach, J., & Buxmann, P. (2011). Investigating the acceptance of electronic books: The impact of haptic dissonance on innovation adoption. *Ecis*, (2011), 1–13.

Ghose, A., Goldfarb, A., & Han, S. P. (2013). How is the mobile internet different? Search costs and local activities. *Information Systems Research*, 24(3), 613–631.

Grohmann, B., Spangenberg, E. R., & Sprott, D. E. (2007). The influence of tactile input on the evaluation of retail product offerings. *Journal of Retailing*, 83(2), 237–245.

Heckman, J. J. (1979). Sample Selection Bias as a Specification Error. *Econometrica, 47*(1), 153.

Hein, W., O'Donohoe, S., & Ryan, A. (2011). Mobile phones as an extension of the participant observer's self. *Qualitative Market Research: An International Journal, 14*(3), 258–273.

Holbrook, M. B. (1978). Beyond Attitude Structure: Toward the Informational Determinants of Attitude. *Journal of Marketing Research, 15*(4), 545.

Jiang, Z., & Benbasat, I. (2005). Virtual Product Experience : Effects of Visual and Functional Control of Products on Perceived Diagnosticity and Flow in Electronic Shopping. *Journal of Management Information Systems, 21*(3), 111–147.

Jiang, Z., & Benbasat, I. (2007). Investigating the influence of the functional mechanisms of online product presentations. *Information Systems Research, 18*(4), 454–470.

Kim, K., Proctor, R. W., & Salvendy, G. (2011). Comparison of 3D and 2D menus for cell phones. *Computers in Human Behavior, 27*(5), 2056–2066.

Klatzky, R. L., Lederman, S. J., & Matula, D. E. (1993). Haptic exploration in the presence of vision. *Journal of Experimental Psychology. Human Perception and Performance.*

Klatzky, R. L., Loomis, J. M., Golledge, R. G., Cicinelli, J. G., Doherty, S., & Pellegrino, J. W. (1990). Acquisition of Route and Survey Knowledge in the Absence of Vision. *Journal of Motor Behavior, 22*(1), 19–43.

Klatzky, R. L., & Peck, J. (2012). Please Touch: Object Properties that Invite Touch. *IEEE Transactions on Haptics, 5*(2), 139–147.

Krämer, F., Schmidt, K. M., Spann, M., & Stich, L. (2017). Delegating pricing power to customers: Pay What You Want or Name Your Own Price? *Journal of Economic Behavior and Organization, 136*, 125–140.

Laroche, M., Yang, Z., McDougall, G. H. G., & Bergeron, J. (2005). Internet versus bricks-and-mortar retailers: An investigation into intangibility and its consequences. *Journal of Retailing, 81*(4), 251–267.

Lederman, S. J., & Klatzky, R. L. (1990). Haptic classification of common objects: Knowledge-driven exploration. *Cognitive Psychology, 22*(4), 421–459.

Li, H., Daugherty, T., & Biocca, F. (2002). Impact of 3-D Advertising on Product Knowledge, Brand Attitude, and Purchase Intention: The Mediating Role of Presence. *Journal of Advertising, 31*(3), 43–57.

McCabe, D. B., & Nowlis, S. M. (2003). The Effect of Examining Actual Products or Product Descriptions on Consumer Preference. *Journal of Consumer Psychology, 13*(4), 431–439.

Mooy, S. C., & Robben, H. S. J. (2002). Managing consumers' product evaluations through direct product experience. *Journal of Product & Brand Management, 11*(7), 432–446.

Peck, J., Barger, V. A., & Webb, A. (2013). In search of a surrogate for touch: The effect of haptic imagery on perceived ownership. *Journal of Consumer Psychology, 23*(2), 189–196.

Peck, J., & Childers, T. L. (2003a). Individual Differences in Haptic Information Processing: The "Need for Touch" Scale. *Journal of Consumer Research*, *30*(3), 430–442.

Peck, J., & Childers, T. L. (2003b). To Have and To Hold: The Influence of Haptic Information on Product Judgments. *Journal of Marketing*, *67*(2), 35–48.

Peck, J., & Shu, S. B. (2009). The Effect of Mere Touch on Perceived Ownership. *Journal of Consumer Research*, *36*(3), 434–447. https://doi.org/10.1086/598614

Pierce, J. L., Kostova, T., & Dirks, K. T. (2001). Toward a Theory of Psychological Ownership in Organizations. *Academy of Management Review*, *26*(2), 298–310.

Pierce, J. L., Kostova, T., & Dirks, K. T. (2003). The state of psychological ownership: Integrating and extending a century of research. *Review of General Psychology*, *7*(1), 84–107.

Preacher, K. J., & Hayes, A. F. (2004). SPSS and SAS procedures for estimating indirect effects in simple mediation models. *Behavior Research Methods, Instruments, & Computers*, *36*(4), 717–731.

Preacher, K. J., & Hayes, A. F. (2008). Asymptotic and resampling strategies for assessing and comparing indirect effects in multiple mediator models. *Behavior Research Methods*, *40*(3), 879–891.

Roggeveen, A. L., Grewal, D., Townsend, C., & Krishnan, R. (2015). The Impact of Dynamic Presentation Format on Consumer Preferences for Hedonic Products and Services. *Journal of Marketing*, *79*(6), 34–49.

Schlosser, A. E. (2003). Experiencing Products in the Virtual World: The Role of Goal and Imagery in Influencing Attitudes versus Purchase Intentions. *Journal of Consumer Research*, *30*(2), 184–198.

Shen, H., Zhang, M., & Krishna, A. (2016). Computer Interfaces and the "Direct-Touch" Effect: Can iPads Increase the Choice of Hedonic Food? *Journal of Marketing Research*, *53*(5), 745–758.

Steuer, J. (1992). Defining Virtual Reality: Dimensions Determining Telepresence. *Journal of Communication*, *42*(4), 73–93.

Streicher, M. C., & Estes, Z. (2016). Multisensory interaction in product choice: Grasping a product affects choice of other seen products. *Journal of Consumer Psychology*, *26*(4), 558–565.

van Dolen, W. M., Dabholkar, P. A., & de Ruyter, K. (2007). Satisfaction with Online Commercial Group Chat: The Influence of Perceived Technology Attributes, Chat Group Characteristics, and Advisor Communication Style. *Journal of Retailing*, *83*(3), 339–358.

Verhagen, T., Vonkeman, C., Feldberg, F., & Verhagen, P. (2014). Present it like it is here: Creating local presence to improve online product experiences. *Computers in Human Behavior*, *39*, 270–280.

Wang, R. J. H., Malthouse, E. C., & Krishnamurthi, L. (2015). On the Go: How Mobile Shopping Affects Customer Purchase Behavior. *Journal of Retailing*, *91*(2), 217–234.

Wang, Z., & Nelson, M. R. (2014). Tablet as human: How intensity and stability of the user-tablet relationship influences users' impression formation of tablet computers. *Computers in Human*

Wood, S. L. (2001). Remote Purchase Environments: The Influence of Return Policy Leniency on Two-Stage Decision Processes. *Journal of Marketing Research, 38*(2), 157–169.

Xu, K., Chan, J., Ghose, A., & Han, S. P. (2017). Battle of the Channels: The Impact of Tablets on Digital Commerce. *Management Science, 63*(5), 1469–1492.

Appendix

Measurement scales in online experiment.

Perceived Textural Fit *(Scale reliability coefficient: .76; adapted from Gerlach and Buxmann, 2011)*
1. Touching the smartphone surface felt similar to touching a real [cork] mug surface.
2. Examining the [cork] mug felt realistic.
3. Examining the [cork] mug felt like touching a real [cork] mug.

Perceived Ownership *(Scale reliability coefficient: .97; adapted from* (Pierce et al., 2001; *2003)*
1. I feel like this is my mug.
2. I feel like I own this mug.
3. I feel a high degree of personal ownership of this mug.

Information Control *(Scale reliability coefficient: .89; adapted from Dabholkar, 1996; van Dolen et al., 2007)*

1. I feel much control over the process when examining the product in this presentation format.
2. This product presentation format gave me direct influence on getting the information I need.
3. This product presentation format enabled me to get a grip on the necessary information.

Autotelic Need for Touch *(Scale reliability coefficient: .86; adapted from Peck and Childers, 2003b)*

1. Touching products can be fun.
2. I like to touch products even if I have no intention of buying them.
3. I find myself touching all kinds of products in stores.

Instrumental Need for Touch *(Scale reliability coefficient: .90; adapted from Peck and Childers, 2003b)*
1. I place more trust in products that can be touched before purchase.
2. I feel more comfortable purchasing a product after physically examining it.
3. I feel more confident making a purchase after touching a product.

V   Article 4

The Effect of Goal-Oriented Mobile User Interfaces on Consumer Attitudes[1]

Abstract

Smartphones are used for many types of product research, which can be broadly categorized into casual browsing and target search. Still, modern mobile web design is responsive to device-related restrictions such as screen size, but does not consider consumer-related characteristics such as goal orientation. Our study addresses the question of how goal-oriented mobile user interface (UI) design affects consumer attitudes towards shopping at the website. In our online experiment comprising 399 observations, we manipulate three factors: *interaction technique* (vertical scrolling vs. horizontal swiping), *screen layout* (one vs. three products displayed simultaneously), and *assortment size* (six vs. 15 products to choose from). Our results show a moderating effect of goal orientation on the relationship between consumer perceptions and attitudes: browsers are primarily driven by enjoyment, whereas searchers tend to put more emphasis on diagnosticity. Furthermore, we demonstrate that assortment size negatively moderates the (otherwise positive) relationship between screen layout and perceived enjoyment: while a screen layout displaying several products simultaneously seems to result in a more joyful experience, this effect is attenuated by increasing assortment size. Third, we examine our eight different treatment groups more closely and discover that consumer attitudes toward different combinations of UI design elements differ substantially, depending on goal orientation. We conclude that goal orientation of individual consumers should play an increasingly important role in mobile user interface design considerations for researchers and practitioners alike.

Keywords: *mobile, interface, UI, user goals, consumer attitudes*

---

[1] This article is based on the following working paper: Naegelein, P., Lachner, F. & Spann, M. (2017). *The Effect of Goal-Oriented Mobile User Interfaces on Consumer Attitudes.* Working Paper. LMU Munich.

1   Introduction

Fueled by the rapid adoption of smartphones and tablets, mobile commerce has been rising steadily over the past decade. As a result, consumers increasingly research and purchase products online on their mobile devices: according to Statista (2017), mobile commerce accounted for more than 20 percent of online sales in the U.S. at the end of 2016 and is predicted to grow to almost 50 percent by 2020. This trend has attracted scholars from many different disciplines such as psychology, marketing, human-computer-interaction and information systems, who address the challenge of designing for virtual product interactions (Verhagen et al., 2014; Roggeveen et al., 2015; Blazquez Cano et al., 2017) and explore the specific capabilities of touch-based mobile devices (Brasel and Gips, 2014; 2015).

According to a consumer survey conducted by Google (2015), smartphones are used for many types of product research. On the one hand, mobile devices are frequently used for casual browsing: 30 percent of respondents reported they were looking for inspiration, another 22 percent regularly discover relevant brands on their mobile phone. On the other hand, mobile devices are frequently used for targeted search: 36 percent compare products, prices, and features on their smartphone, while 22 percent seek opinions, review, or advice.

There is no constantly preferred type of product research for any individual, since overarching consumer goals such as browsing or searching mostly depend on situational factors (Endsley and Jones, 2012). Still, modern mobile web design is responsive to device-related restrictions such as screen size, but does not consider consumer-related characteristics such as goal orientation. Hence, the central research question guiding our work is how goal-oriented mobile user interface design influences consumer attitudes. We root this study in the literature streams on consumer goals and mobile user interface design.

Consumer goals. When consumers shop for products and services online, their goal-setting largely falls into two broad categories. While *searchers* primarily aim to retrieve relevant product information for decision-making, *browsers* tend to care more about having a joyful, entertaining experience (Hoffman and Novak, 1996; Janiszewski, 1998). Moe (2003) classifies shopping strategies along two dimensions: *search behavior* could be directed or exploratory, whereas the *purchasing horizon* could be immediate or future-related. Within this context, exploratory search patterns spur casual browsing behavior and correspond to hedonic utilities (Brucks, 1985). Directed buying, in contrast, relates to the search for targeted information and can be viewed as rather utilitarian dimension. Since both types of product research can lead to a product purchase (Moe, 2003), we argue that consumer goals should play a more prominent role in user-centered interface design.

Mobile user interface design. One of the key elements of interactive systems is the user interface (UI), which allows consumers to control a system and interact with it. Research in the field of digital UI discusses not only graphical user interfaces (e.g., Ludolph and Perkins, 1998) but also touch-based and tangible interfaces as well as voice and gesture interaction. While gesture interaction has so far only been established in niche application areas and lacks a common understanding of effective design (Liu and Thomas, 2017), voice interaction on mobile phones is often used to complement touch-based interaction techniques (Corbett and Weber, 2016). At the same time, touch screens provide a strong appeal to users and have become a key component of smartphones (Benko et al., 2006; Blazquez Cano et al., 2017). The field of mobile UI design faces the specific challenge to adapt layout, design, and interaction mechanisms to smaller screen sizes of handheld devices (Nilsson, 2009; Ghose et al., 2013). As a consequence, most developers pursue a responsive design approach that allows the interface to automatically adapt to the size and medium of a device (Mullins, 2015). Hartmann et al. (2007), however, demonstrate that aesthetics and usability of interfaces are dependent on consumer goals. Similarly, Cooper et al. (2014) highlight that goal-oriented design represents individual mental models best. These findings and paradigms from consumer psychology and human-computer interaction serve as a basis for designing mobile user interfaces tailored to consumer goals.

Our study provides two main contributions. First, we show that goal orientation significantly affects consumer perceptions: while browsers are primarily influenced by enjoyment, searchers mostly care about diagnosticity. Second, we illustrate that consumer attitudes toward certain mobile UI design combinations differ significantly depending on goal orientation.

The remainder of this work is organized as follows: in Section 2, we derive our hypotheses from theory on consumer psychology, information systems, and human-computer interaction. Then, in Section 3, we describe the method, sample and design of our online experiment, followed by the results of our statistical analysis in Section 4. To conclude, we provide a general discussion of the results and derive theoretical and managerial implications as well as avenues for further research.

2   Theory and Development of Hypotheses

In the following, we outline the theoretical framework of this study and derive our hypotheses. Our research model, depicted in Figure 1, builds upon a cognitive-affective view of consumer behavior. One the one hand, following the expectancy-value model, evaluative judgments can be seen as an inevitable, effortless consequence of cognitive processes (Feather, 1982; Fishbein, 1963; Fishbein and Ajzen, 1975). On the other hand, the affective-primacy hypothesis would suggest that affect dominates cognition (Zajonc, 1980). Meanwhile, most scholars have embraced a multi-component conceptualization which views both affect and cognition as competing but similarly important determinants of consumer attitude (Ajzen, 2001; Eagly and Chaiken, 1993; van der Pligt et al., 1997). Research on the effects of digital interactions mechanisms, for instance, oftentimes discusses the mediating effects of perceived enjoyment and diagnosticity (e.g., Jiang and Benbasat, 2007; Kim and Forsythe, 2008; Verhagen et al., 2014). In our work, we investigate the two UI elements *interaction technique* (vertical scroll vs. horizontal swipe) and *screen layout* (one product vs. three products displayed simultaneously). These two dimensions represent mobile UI elements which are substantially different from traditional web-based interfaces on desktop computers and adapt to the limited screen size and touch-enabled display technology of smartphones (Raneburger et al., 2013). Furthermore, we consider these elements as crucial for goal-oriented mobile interface design based on consumer motivations and needs, contrasting current responsive design strategies that base interface adaption primarily on a medium's screen size.

Figure 1. Research Model.

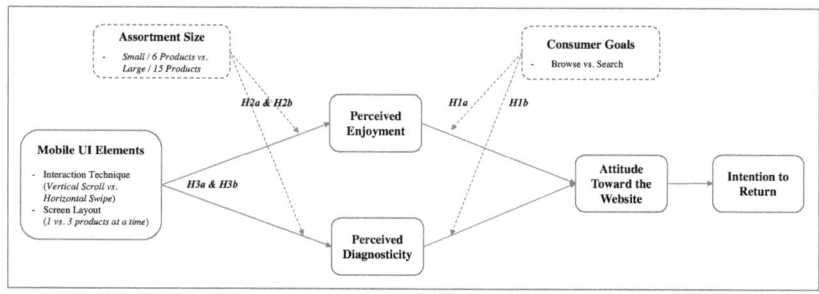

2.1   The Moderating Effect of Consumer Goals

As a starting point for our evaluation of mobile user interfaces, we need to understand to which degree consumers' goal orientation influences relative importance of affect and cognition. For instance, Schlosser (2003) demonstrates that goal-oriented interaction design can affect consumer attitudes: browsers were shown to hold more favorable attitudes when exposed to an object-interactive website relative to a static website. Searchers, in contrast, could rather be persuaded by passively delivered information in static, text-based formats.

Detlor et al. (2003) show that browsers value personal components signaling higher levels of trust such as information about the retailer, whereas searchers place greater emphasis on more detailed product information. Furthermore, Schlosser (2006) finds a moderating effect of consumer goals on online purchase decisions. Taken together, these findings suggest that during product evaluation, browsers might be rather persuaded by an entertaining interactive experience (corresponding to perceived enjoyment), whereas searchers require more information to mitigate product-level uncertainty (corresponding to perceived diagnosticity). Thus, we hypothesize:

H1a: *Browsing goals (relative to search goals) positively moderate the relationship between perceived enjoyment and consumer attitudes.*

H1b: *Browsing goals (relative to search goals) negatively moderate the relationship between perceived diagnosticity and consumer attitudes.*

2.2   The Moderating Effect of Assortment Size

For a long time, literature on assortment size almost unequivocally argued that greater choice was always better (Oppewal and Koelemeijer, 2005). In recent years, however, more and more scholars have challenged the idea that choosing from more alternatives has to be more desirable: Diehl and Poynor (2010) observe reduced consumer satisfaction with increasing assortment size. Similarly, Sela et al. (2009) find that choosing from larger assortment can be oftentimes more challenging and difficult. In particular when products differ along multiple dimensions, increasing variety could backfire. Gourville and Soman (2005) refer to this phenomenon as "overchoice" and show that this effect could be reversed, among others, through simplified information presentation. In summary, we expect:

H2a: *An increasing assortment size negatively moderates the effect of horizontal swipe interaction (relative to vertical scroll interaction) on perceived enjoyment and diagnosticity.*

H2b: *An increasing assortment size negatively moderates the effect of screen layout (multiple products shown simultaneously relative to one) on perceived enjoyment and diagnosticity.*

2.3   The Mediating Effect of Perceived Enjoyment and Diagnosticity

Interaction technique. Horizontal and vertical scrolling became key features on mobile phones as touchscreens allow for input modalities beyond clicking and tapping (Cooper et al., 2014). Balagtas-Fernandez et al. (2009) demonstrate that users prefer scrolling compared to tapping on handheld devices, whereas Nilsson (2009) suggests minimizing horizontal gestures in favor of vertical scrolling to avoid information loss. However, Cooper et al. (2014) argue that while there are some benefits of vertical scrolling when presenting text and text lists, horizontal interaction becomes more relevant with increasing visual content. Within the mobile app industry, there is a clear trend towards applications that use swipe gestures as their main interaction technique – prominent examples include online dating (e.g., *Tinder*), job search (e.g., *jobr*), or mobile shopping (e.g., *Kwoller*). Similarly, Dou and Sundar (2016) find positive effects of swiping techniques on behavioral intentions. We hypothesize that the effect on consumer attitudes is mediated by both an affective and cognitive dimension:

H3a: *Interaction Technique: The effect of horizontal swipe interfaces (relative to vertical scroll interfaces) on consumer attitudes is fully mediated through perceived enjoyment and perceived diagnosticity.*

Screen Layout. Adapting web interfaces to smaller screen sizes of handheld devices such as smartphones requires content to be reduced and information to be presented in a more concise manner (cf. Ghose et al., 2013). With multimedia technologies advancing, not only textual but also visual cues have become widely available in online store settings (Verhagen et al., 2014). Mobile interface designers, thus, need to continuously balance the size of pictures on the one side, and the number of products presented simultaneously on the other side. The overall goal of combining text and visuals is to ensure a pleasant readability and reduce erroneous selections (Warr and Chi, 2013). In addition, the number of required user interactions to explore all products rises significantly with increasing assortment sizes. Within this context, Chae and Kim (2004) show that smaller screens make it more difficult for users to relocate their reference point while analyzing content on mobile phones, as content on the screen is constantly changing. Generally, there is consensus among interface designers that the number of required interactions should be minimized to ensure a pleasant user experience (Cooper et al., 2014). Besides such rather hedonic aspects, there is a more cognitive rationale as well: since humans' short-term memory capacity is limited (Miller, 1956), Shneiderman et al. (2016) argue that the number of different interface pages should be reduced to a minimum so that users do not need to remember information from previous pages. Hence, we hypothesize:

H3b: *Screen Layout: The effect of showing multiple products at a time (relative to showing only one product at a time) on consumer attitudes is fully mediated through perceived enjoyment and perceived diagnosticity.*

3   Online Experiment

To address our research question, we ran an online experiment using Amazon Mechanical Turk (AMT). Our sample consists of 399 respondents from who completed the task on their mobile phones. All participants are based in the U.S. and familiar with mobile shopping (average self-reported familiarity with shopping on smartphones of $\mu = 6.26$ on a scale from *1 / not familiar at all* to *7 / very familiar*, see Table 1). The sample is fairly evenly split in terms of gender (54 percent female, 46 percent male) and covers a broad age range from 18 to 87 years (average: $\mu = 32.79$ years). Our participants were presented with a shopping scenario and asked to choose their favorite mug from the assortment presented in our experimental online store. Thereafter, they answered a set of questions via an online survey displayed on the same device. Beforehand, we had informed the participants that at the end of the survey, they would have the chance to participate in a lottery (on a voluntary basis) and win their chosen mug.

Table 1. Summary statistics.

Variable	Mean	Std. Dev.	Min	Max
Interaction Technique (DV[a])	.48	.50	0	1
Screen Layout (DV[b])	.49	.50	0	1
Assortment Size (DV[c])	.51	.50	0	1
Goal (DV[d])	.76	.43	0	1
Perceived Diagnosticity	5.08	1.30	1	7
Perceived Enjoyment	5.11	1.28	1	7
Attitude toward the Website	5.38	1.28	1	7
Intention to Return	5.15	1.39	1	7
Age (in years)	32.79	9.05	18	87
Gender (DV[e])	.46	.50	0	1
Familiarity	6.26	1.20	1	7

N = 399 observations. DV: Dummy variable. a: 0 = vertical scroll, 1 = horizontal swipe. b: 0 = one product shown simultaneously, 1 = three products shown simultaneously. c: 0 = small assortment, 1 = large assortment. d: 0 = search goal, 1 = browse goal. e: 0 = female, 1 = male.

Experimental manipulation. Our experiment consists of a 2 (*interaction technique*: vertical scrolling vs. horizontal swiping) x 2 (*screen layout*: one vs. three products shown simultaneously) x 2 *(assortment size*: small vs. large) design, with the three factors manipulated between subjects. With regard to assortment size, we presented six products in the "small assortment" condition (the minimum number of products required to have at least one screen change through scrolling or swiping when three products are shown at the same time) and 15 products in the "large assortment" condition. This setting leads to our sample consisting of eight different treatment groups (see Table 2 as well as Figure 2).

Table 2. Overview of treatment groups.

Group	Interaction Technique	Screen Layout	Assortment Size	Group Size		
				Total	*Browsers*	*Searchers*
#1	vertical scroll	one product	small	49	34	15
#2	vertical scroll	one product	large	53	42	11
#3	vertical scroll	three products	small	52	40	12
#4	vertical scroll	three products	large	52	41	11
#5	horizontal swipe	one product	small	47	34	13
#6	horizontal swipe	one product	large	53	38	15
#7	horizontal swipe	three products	small	47	36	11
#8	horizontal swipe	three products	large	46	38	8
SUM				*399*	*303*	*96*

Figure 2. Online experiment: screenshots of (a) vertical scrolling and one product shown at a time; (b) vertical scrolling and three products shown at a time; (c) horizontal swiping and one product shown at a time; (d) horizontal swiping and three products shown at a time.

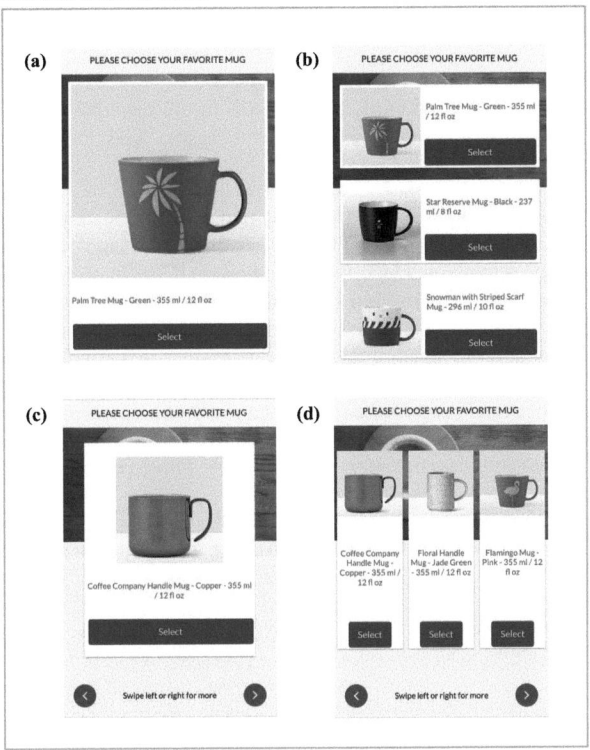

Measurement. The overall goal of this work is to study the effects of goal-oriented interface design. Hence, we chose consumers' *attitude toward shopping at the website* as key dependent variable in our research model. This construct, based on Grazioli and Jarvenpaa (2000) as well as Coyle and Thorson (2001) is based on a three-item, seven-point Likert-type scale (detailed measures of constructs as well as scale reliabilities are reported in the appendix). Attitudes have been shown to be an antecedent of intentions (Fishbein 1967; Ajzen and Fishbein, 1977). Hence, we measure consumers' *intention to return to the website* as well (Coyle and Thorson, 2001). Our mediating variables are *perceived diagnosticity* (Jiang and Benbasat 2005, 2007) and *perceived enjoyment* (Koufaris, 2002; Jiang and Benbasat, 2007). Furthermore, we asked our participants about their *goal orientation*, i.e., whether their goal was rather targeted search or casual browsing when they were choosing their preferred mug. Finally, we collected data about their age, gender, and familiarity with mobile shopping as control variables.

4   Results

In this section, we first show a path analysis investigating the proposed moderators and mediators, followed by a comparison of our eight treatment groups through parametric and non-parametric tests.

4.1   Analysis of Moderators and Mediators

To analyze the mediating and moderating effects in our research model, we conduct an observed variable path analysis (Preacher and Hayes, 2004; Hayes, 2013) for each of our two UI elements.

Interaction technique. Figure 3 illustrates the path analysis for interaction technique as independent variable. We find that large parts of the variance in consumer attitude toward the website is explained by our two mediators ($R^2 = .75$). Specifically, attitudes are strongly influenced by perceived enjoyment (path coefficient = .78; $p < .01$) and, to a much lesser extent, by perceived diagnosticity (path coefficient = .16, $p < .05$). Both are moderated by consumer goals (modeled as dummy variable, with search goal = 0 and browse goal = 1): we observe a positive moderating effect of browse goals on the relationship between perceived enjoyment and attitude (path coefficient = .22; $p < .01$), and a negative moderating effect on the relationship between perceived diagnosticity and attitude (path coefficient = -.22; $p < .01$). Thus, Hypotheses 1a and 1b are supported.

Figure 3. Path analysis for interaction technique as independent variable.

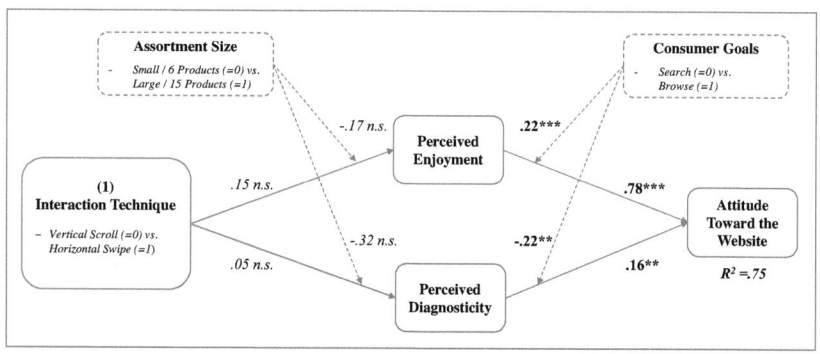

****p<.01*, ** *p<.05*, * *p<.10*

However, we do not find any significant moderating effects of assortment size (modeled as dummy variable, with small assortment = 0 and large assortment = 1) for the relationship between interaction technique and perceived enjoyment (path coefficient = -.17; $p > .10$) or perceived diagnosticity (path coefficient = -.32; $p > .10$).

Hence, Hypothesis 2a is not supported. Furthermore, there are no significant paths supporting a mediating effect of perceived enjoyment (path coefficient = .15; p > .10) or perceived diagnosticity (path coefficient = .05; p > .10). Hypothesis 3a is, thus, not supported.

Screen layout. The path analysis for screen layout as independent variable is depicted in Figure 4. Again, we observe that similarly large parts of the variance in consumer attitudes are explained by our mediators (R^2 = .75) and find almost identical effects for perceived enjoyment (path coefficient = .78; p < .01) and perceived diagnosticity (path coefficient = .15, p < .05). Also, consumer goals appear to be a consistent moderator of the relationship between perception and attitude, indicated by a positive moderation effect for enjoyment (path coefficient = .22; p < .05), and a negative moderation effect for diagnosticity (path coefficient = -.22; p < .05). Hypothesis 1a and 1b are supported once more.

Figure 4. Path analysis for screen layout as independent variable.

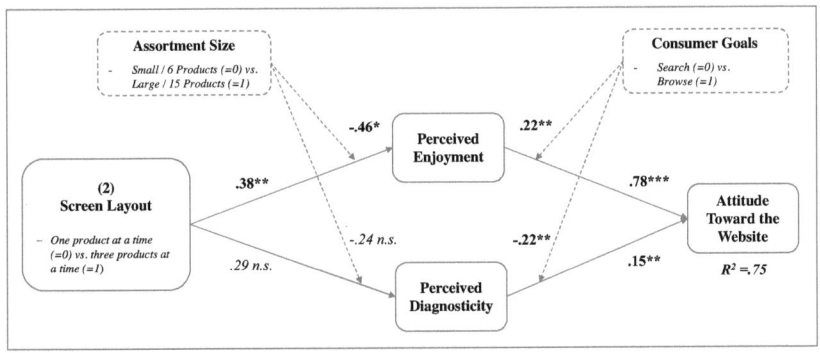

*** p<.01, ** p<.05, * p<.10

In contrast to our previous analysis, we do find a moderating effect of assortment size. More precisely, we observe a significant, negative moderating effect for the relationship between screen layout and perceived enjoyment (path coefficient = .46; p < .10). The moderating effect for the relationship between screen layout and perceived diagnosticity, however, remains insignificant (path coefficient = -.24; p > .10). Hence, Hypothesis 2b is partially supported. Moreover, our model reveals perceived enjoyment as mediator (path coefficient = .38; p < .05) for screen layout, whereas we don't find a similar significant effect for perceived diagnosticity (path coefficient = .29; p < .10). Hypothesis 3b, thus, is partially supported. Finally, we examine the path between attitudes and intentions to return. An OLS regression indicates a strong and significant relationship (coefficient = 0.92, p < .01), with large parts of the variance explained (R^2 = .73).

4.2 Analysis of UI Elements and Consumer Goals

Our 2 (*interaction technique*: vertical scrolling vs. horizontal swiping) x 2 (*screen layout*: one vs. three products shown simultaneously) x 2 *(assortment size*: six vs. 15 different products to choose from) factorial design led to a total of eight different treatment groups. Figure 5 provides an overview of how arithmetic means for consumer attitude differ between groups, in particular when factoring in consumer goals: the solid black line represents the overall sample, whereas the dashed line depicts means for the subsample of browsers only, and the dotted line illustrates the subsample of searchers only.

Figure 5. Arithmetic means for consumer attitudes, clustered by treatment group.

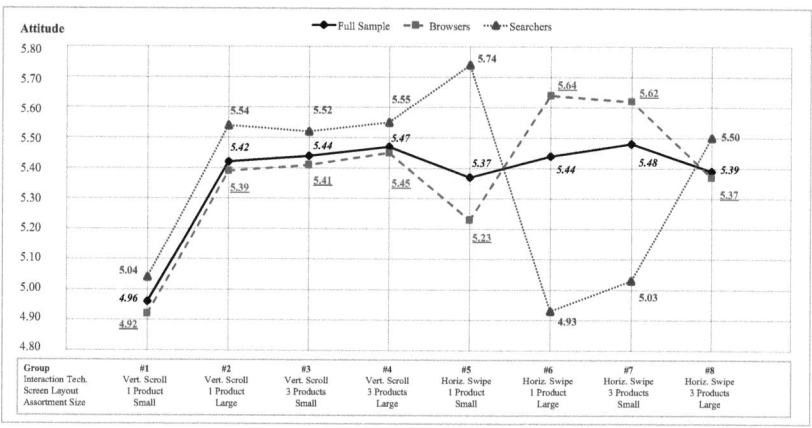

First, we take a closer look at the full sample (solid line, mean values in italics). We chose Group #1 (μ_1 = 4.96) as baseline since it is characterized by vertical scrolling, one product shown at a time, and a small assortment size – arguably one of the most frequently used setups to be found when visiting online stores on mobile phones. It becomes apparent that relative to Group #1, our baseline, all other combinations lead to a significantly higher means for consumers' attitude towards shopping at the website (see Table 3a). All arithmetic means of Group #2 to #8 fall into a narrow corridor ranging from μ_5 = 5.37 (Δ = .42; p > .10) for Group #5 to μ_7 = 5.48 (Δ = .48; p < .05) for Group #7.

Table 3a. Mean differences of consumer attitude between treatment groups (full sample; two-sample t-tests with equal variances).

	Group (I)	Group (J)	Mean Diff. (I -J)	Sig.		Std. Err.	95% Confidence Interval	
		Group 2	.46	.084	*	.265	-.063	.987
		Group 3	.48	.074	*	.268	-.048	1.015
		Group 4	.51	.069	*	.277	-.041	1.059
Full Sample	*Baseline: Group 1 (Attitude Mean: 4.95)*	Group 5	.42	.129		.272	-.124	.957
		Group 6	.48	.086	*	.277	-.069	1.031
		Group 7	.53	.032	**	.244	.046	1.101
		Group 8	.44	.098	*	.263	-.082	.961

Total N = 399 / Two-sample t-tests with equal variances / *** p<.01, ** p<.05, * p<.10

As illustrated in Figure 5, splitting the sample by goal orientation yields some surprising insights. Group #1 to #4, all characterized by the interaction technique of vertical scroll, show a consistent pattern, with browsers' attitudes always slightly above the respective full sample average, and searchers' attitudes always slightly below. This picture changes, however, when horizontal swipe comes into play: for both our subsamples, mean values start to diverge into both directions.

Second, thus, we examine the subsample of browsers more closely. As illustrated by the dashed line in Figure 5, mean values for browsers tend to lie slightly below full sample average. However, there are two exceptions: Group #6 (μ_{6B} = 5.64; Δ = .72; p < .05) and Group #7 (μ_{6B} = 5.62; Δ = .71; p < .05) perform not only significantly better than baseline Group #1, but also relative to searchers. All mean differences for browsers are summarized in Table 3b.

Table 3b. Mean differences of consumer attitude between treatment groups (browsers only; two sample t-tests with equal variances).

Group (I)	Group (J)	Mean Diff. (I -J)	Sig.		Std. Err.	95% Confidence Interval	
		Group 2	.47	.147		.319	-.167	1.102
		Group 3	.50	.128		.322	-.146	1.136
Goal: Browsing	*Baseline: Group 1 (Attitude Mean: 4.92)*	Group 4	.53	.120		.334	-.139	1.191
		Group 5	.31	.350		.333	-.352	.979
		Group 6	.72	.024	**	.311	.098	1.340
		Group 7	.71	.017	**	.290	.129	1.287
		Group 8	.46	.148		.312	-.166	1.077

*Total N = 303 / Two-sample t-tests with equal variances / *** p<.01, ** p<.05, * p<.10*

Third, we investigate the subsample of searchers. Please note that out of our full sample, less than a quarter of participants indicated their main goal was to search (see Table 2). Hence, our treatment groups comprise no more than eight to 15 observations. To account for these small group sizes, we conducted Wilcoxon rank-sum tests to analyze mean differences. While no significant effects were found (see Table 3c), Figure 5 (dotted line) points at stark contrasts that might materialize with increasing sample size. Most notably, we observe the highest of all attitude scores for searchers in Group #5 (μ_{5S} = 5.74; Δ = .70; p > .10) and one of the lowest in Group #6 (μ_{6S} = 4.93; Δ = -.11; p > .10).

Table 3c. Mean differences of consumer attitude between treatment groups (searchers only; Wilcoxon rank-sum test).

Group (I)		Group (J)	Mean Diff. (I -J)	Sig.	Std. Err	95% Confidence Interval	
Goal: Searching	Baseline: Group 1 (Attitude Mean: 5.04)	Group 2	.50	.361	.492	-.515	1.517
		Group 3	.48	.280	.502	-.551	1.518
		Group 4	.50	.220	.516	-.563	1.565
		Group 5	.70	.104	.470	-.267	1.665
		Group 6	-.11	.884	.569	-1.277	1.055
		Group 7	-.01	1.000	.449	-.941	.913
		Group 8	.46	.381	.523	-.632	1.543

*Total N = 96 / Wilcoxon rank-sum test / *** p<.01, ** p<.05, * p<.10*

In particular, for groups characterized by horizontal swipe interaction, arithmetic means of consumer attitudes differ substantially between browsers and searchers: $\Delta =$ .51 ($\mu_{5S} = 5.74$; $\mu_{5B} = 5.23$) for Group #5, $\Delta = .71$ ($\mu_{6S} = 4.93$; $\mu_{6B} = 5.64$) for Group 6, and $\Delta = .59$ ($\mu_{6S} = 5.03$; $\mu_{6B} = 5.62$) for Group #6. These observations provide additional support for the consideration of consumers' goal orientation when designing mobile user interfaces and are further discussed in Section 5.

5   General Discussion and Conclusion

5.1   Summary and Key Findings

This study examines the role of goal orientation in user interface design. We conducted an online experiment with 399 participants and manipulated three factors: interaction technique, screen layout, and assortment size. Our follow-up survey and subsequent statistical analyses reveal three main findings. First, we show that goal orientation moderates the relationship between consumer perceptions and attitudes. Browsers are primarily driven by enjoyment, whereas searchers tend to put more emphasis on diagnosticity. Second, we demonstrate that assortment size negatively moderates the (otherwise positive) relationship between screen layout and perceived enjoyment. While a screen layout displaying several products simultaneously seems to result in a more joyful experience, this effect is countered by increasing assortment size. Third, we examine our eight different treatment groups more closely and discover that consumer attitudes toward different combinations of UI elements differ substantially, depending on goal orientation. This is particularly the case for store designs based on the interaction technique of horizontal swipe – a more and more frequently used control mechanism in industrial practice.

5.2   Theoretical Implications

Building upon the cognitive-affective framework (Ajzen, 2001), we find - similar to Jiang and Benbasat (2007) - that consumer attitudes are significantly influenced by both perceived diagnosticity and enjoyment. The main contribution of this study is the integration of consumer goals, since prior literature on the role of goal orientation has mainly focused on information processing, customized web search, and promotional messages (Schlosser, 2003; Rose and Levinson, 2004; Moe, 2003). Our results suggest a positive moderating effect of browsing goals on the relation between perceived enjoyment and attitude, and at the same time a negative moderating effect on the relation between perceived diagnosticity and attitude. These findings complement usability studies within the field of human-computer interaction, which oftentimes stress the role of situation awareness in user-centered interface design (Endsley and Jones, 2012). Moreover, similar to Gourville and Soman (2005), we find that simplified information representation - in our case through a screen layout that shows multiple products at once and allows for quick comparisons - positively affects enjoyment. The negative moderating effect of increasing assortment size on consumer attitudes is in line with more recent findings in marketing literature (e.g., Sela et al., 2009; Diehl and Poynor, 2010). Furthermore, we demonstrate that consumer attitudes for certain user interface diverge between browsers and searchers. These observations could be explained by the individual nature of mobile UI, which is subject to varying usage patterns and individual preferences (Gong and Tarasewich, 2004). Therefore, mobile UI designers are presented with the continuous challenge to find a suitable balance between hedonic and ergonomic UI quality instead of maximizing single design elements (cf. Hassenzahl et al., 2000).

5.3   Managerial Implications

For managers and mobile UI developers, our findings are a further step into the direction of disentangling the complexity of user-centered interface design. Above all, the goal-orientation of consumers has one central implication: there is no single superior design solution that fits everybody at any time. Since goal orientation for every individual consumer is dependent on his or her current situation (Endsley and Jones, 2012), it is advisable that mobile user interfaces do not only adapt to technological restrictions such as smaller screens, but also to current behavioral needs of consumers.

5.4   Limitations and Future Research

Our study is subject to some limitations which also provide opportunities for future research. We manipulated two essential design elements, interaction technique and screen layout. However, mobile UI design and its resulting user experience are subject to a variety of factors affecting the look, feel and usability of a web interface (Lachner et al., 2016). Hence, there might be a variety of additional design elements worth exploring. Moreover, our findings are restricted to a comparably small set of observations based on survey data. In our experiment, we collected data on consumer goals after task completion instead of trying to induce goal direction. However, this approach comes at the cost of an unbalanced sample with 75.9 percent browsers and only 24.1 percent searchers. Larger datasets in future studies would allow for a much more granular analysis of differences between single treatment groups. Furthermore, we could not control for context of use in our online experiment. In contrast to desktop computers, which were developed as stationary working stations, mobile devices are typically used in a variety of environments and hence subject to different contextual factors (Kim et al., 2002; Gong and Tarasewich, 2004; Cooper et al., 2014). For instance, our participants might have completed the shopping task and the follow-up survey at home, while commuting, or during a break at work – perceptions, attitudes and goal direction might have been influenced by several unobserved situational factors. Future studies based on empirical data from field experiments could thus provide additional insights regarding mutual dependencies of goal orientation, context of use, and consumer attitudes.

During our experiment, we explicitly asked consumers whether their goal was rather targeted search or casual browsing. As an increasing number of mobile devices (such as the Samsung Galaxy Note 8 or the iPhone X; Bloomberg, 2017) are equipped with face recognition technology, there will be more and more possibilities to measure consumers' mood and emotions. In the near future, we expect that such information will allow for much more subtle and seamless adaptations of mobile user interfaces to consumer goals in real-time. Against this background, the findings of our study suggest that goal orientation of individual consumers should play an increasingly important role in mobile user interface design considerations for researchers and practitioners alike.

References

Ajzen, I. (2001). Nature and Operation of Attitudes. *Annual Review of Psychology*, *52*(1), 27–58.

Balagtas-Fernandez, F., Forrai, J., & Hussmann, H. (2009). Evaluation of user interface design and input methods for applications on mobile touch screen devices. *IFIP Conference on Human-Computer Interaction* (pp. 243-246). Springer.

Benko, H., Wilson, A. D., & Baudisch, P. (2006, April). Precise selection techniques for multi-touch screens. In *Proceedings of the SIGCHI conference on Human Factors in computing systems* (pp. 1263-1272). ACM.

Blazquez Cano, M., Perry, P., Ashman, R., & Waite, K. (2017). The influence of image interactivity upon user engagement when using mobile touch screens. *Computers in Human Behavior*, 1–7.

Bloomberg. (2017). Why iPhone X Face Recognition Is Cool and Creepy. Retrieved September 18, 2017, from https://www.bloomberg.com/news/articles/2017-09-15/why-iphone-x-face-recognition-is-cool-and-creepy-quicktake-q-a.

Brasel, S. A., & Gips, J. (2014). Tablets, touchscreens, and touchpads: How varying touch interfaces trigger psychological ownership and endowment. *Journal of Consumer Psychology*, *24*(2), 226–233.

Brasel, S. A., & Gips, J. (2015). Interface Psychology: Touchscreens Change Attribute Importance, Decision Criteria, and Behavior in Online Choice. *Cyberpsychology, Behavior, and Social Networking*, *18*(9), 534–538.

Brucks, M. (1985). The Effects of Product Class Knowledge on Information Search Behavior. *Journal of Consumer Research*, *12*(1), 1–16.

Chae, M., & Kim, J. (2004). Do size and structure matter to mobile users? An empirical study of the effects of screen size, information structure, and task complexity on user activities with standard web phones. *Behaviour & Information Technology*, *23*(3), 165–181.

Cooper, A., Reimann, R., Cronin, D., & Noessel, C. (2014). *About Face. The Essentials of Interaction Design* (Fourth Edition). John Wiley & Sons.

Corbett, E., & Weber, A. (2016). What can I say? *Proceedings of the 18th International Conference on Human-Computer Interaction with Mobile Devices and Services - MobileHCI '16*, 72–82.

Detlor, B., Sproule, S., & Gupta, C. (2003). Pre-purchase online information seeking: Search versus browse. *Journal of Electronic Commerce Research*, *4*(2), 72–84.

Diehl, K., & Poynor, C. (2010). Great Expectations?! Assortment Size, Expectations, and Satisfaction. *Journal of Marketing Research*, *47*(2), 312–322.

Dou, X., & Sundar, S. S. (2016). Power of the Swipe: Why Mobile Websites Should Add Horizontal Swiping to Tapping, Clicking, and Scrolling Interaction Techniques. *International Journal of Human-Computer Interaction*, *32*(4), 352–362.

Eagly, A. H., & Chaiken, S. (1993). *The psychology of attitudes*. Harcourt Brace Jovanovich College.

Endsley, M. R., & Jones, D. G. (2012). *Designing for situation awareness : an approach to user-centered design*. CRC Press.

Feather, N. (1982). *Expectations and actions: Expectancy-value models in psychology*. Lawrence Erlbaum Associates.

Fishbein, M. (1963). An Investigation of the Relationships between Beliefs about an Object and the Attitude toward that Object. *Human Relations, 16*(3), 233–239.

Fishbein, M., & Ajzen, I. (1975). Belief, attitude, intention and behavior: An introduction to theory and research.

Ghose, A., Goldfarb, A., & Han, S. P. (2013). How is the mobile internet different? Search costs and local activities. *Information Systems Research, 24*(3), 613–631.

Gong, J., & Tarasewich, P. (2004). Guidelines for handheld mobile device interface design. *Proceedings of DSI 2004 Annual Meeting*, 3751–3756.

Google. (2015). What kind of product research did people do on their smartphones? Retrieved September 13, 2017, from https://www.consumerbarometer.com/en/graph-builder/?question=S38&filter=country:united_states.

Gourville, J. T., & Soman, D. (2005). Overchoice and Assortment Type: When and Why Variety Backfires. *Marketing Science, 24*(3), 382–395.

Hartmann, J., Sutcliffe, A., & De Angeli, A. (2007). Investigating attractiveness in web user interfaces. *Proceedings of the SIGCHI Conference on Human Factors in Computing Systems - CHI '07*, 387.

Hassenzahl, M., Platz, A., Burmester, M., & Lehner, K. (2000). Hedonic and ergonomic quality aspects determine a software's appeal. *Proceedings of the SIGCHI Conference on Human Factors in Computing Systems CHI 00, 2*(1), 201–208. ACM.

Hayes, A. F. (2013). *Introduction to mediation, moderation, and conditional process analysis*. Guilford Press.

Hoffman, D. L., & Novak, T. P. (1996). Marketing in Hypermedia Environment Foundations: Conceptual Foundations. *Journal of Marketing, 60*(3), 50–68.

Janiszewski, C. (1998). The Influence of Display Characteristics on Visual Exploratory Search Behavior. *Journal of Consumer Research, 25*(3), 290–301.

Jiang, Z., & Benbasat, I. (2007). Investigating the influence of the functional mechanisms of online product presentations. *Information Systems Research, 18*(4), 454–470.

Kim, H., Kim, J., Lee, Y., Chae, M., & Choi, Y. (2002). An empirical study of the use contexts and usability problems in mobile Internet. *System Sciences, 2002. HICSS. Proceedings of the 35th Annual Hawaii International Conference on* (pp. 1767-1776). IEEE.

Kim, J., & Forsythe, S. (2008). Adoption of Virtual Try-on technology for online apparel shopping. *Journal of Interactive Marketing, 22*(2), 45–59.

Lachner, F., Naegelein, P., Kowalski, R., Spann, M., & Butz, A. (2016). Quantified UX: Towards a Common Organizational Understanding of User Experience. *Proceedings of the 9th Nordic Conference on Human-Computer Interaction - NordiCHI '16*, 1–10. ACM.

Liu, X., & Thomas, G. W. (2017). Gesture Interfaces: Minor Change in Effort, Major Impact on Appeal. In *Proceedings of the 2017 CHI Conference on Human Factors in Computing Systems - CHI '17* (pp. 4278–4283). ACM Press.

Ludolph, F., & Perkins, R. (1998). The Lisa User Interface. *CHI 98 Conference Summary on Human Factors in Computing Systems* (pp. 18–19). ACM

Miller, G. A. (1956). The magical number seven, plus or minus two: some limits on our capacity for processing information. *Psychological Review, 63*(2), 81–97.

Moe, W. W. (2003). Buying , Searching , or Browsing : Differentiating Between Online Shoppers Using In-Store Navigational Clickstream. *Journal of Consumer Psychology, 13*(2000), 29–39.

Mullins, C. (2015). Responsive, Mobile App, Mobile First: Untangling the UX Design Web in Practical Experience. *Proceedings of the 33rd Annual International Conference on the Design of Communication (SIGDOC '15)*, 22:1-22:6.

Nilsson, E. G. (2009). Design patterns for user interface for mobile applications. *Advances in Engineering Software, 40*(12), 1318–1328.

Oppewal, H., & Koelemeijer, K. (2005). More choice is better: Effects of assortment size and composition on assortment evaluation. *International Journal of Research in Marketing, 22*(1), 45–60.

Preacher, K. J., & Hayes, A. F. (2004). SPSS and SAS procedures for estimating indirect effects in simple mediation models. *Behavior Research Methods, Instruments, & Computers, 36*(4), 717–731.

Raneburger, D., Popp, R., Alonso-Ríos, D., Kaindl, H., & Falb, J. (2013). A user study with GUIs tailored for smartphones and tablet PCs. *Proceedings - 2013 IEEE International Conference on Systems, Man, and Cybernetics, SMC 2013* (pp. 3727–3732). Springer.

Roggeveen, A. L., Grewal, D., Townsend, C., & Krishnan, R. (2015). The Impact of Dynamic Presentation Format on Consumer Preferences for Hedonic Products and Services. *Journal of Marketing, 79*(6), 34–49.

Rose, D. E., & Levinson, D. (2004). Understanding User Goals in Web Search. *Proceedings of the 13th international conference on World Wide Web*, New York, NY, USA.

Schlosser, A. E. (2003). Experiencing Products in the Virtual World: The Role of Goal and Imagery in Influencing Attitudes versus Purchase Intentions. *Journal of Consumer Research, 30*(2), 184–198.

Schlosser, A. E., White, T. B., & Lloyd, S. M. (2006). Converting Web Site Visitors into Buyers: How Web Site Investment Increases Consumer Trusting Beliefs and Online Purchase Intentions. *Journal of Marketing, 70*(2), 133–148.

Sela, A., Berger, J., & Liu, W. (2009). Variety, Vice, and Virtue: How Assortment Size Influences Option Choice. *Journal of Consumer Research, 35*(6), 941–951.

Shneiderman, B., Plaisant, C., Cohen, M. S., Jacobs, S., Elmqvist, N., & Diakopoulos, N. (2016). *Designing the user interface: strategies for effective human-computer interaction.* Pearson.

Statista. (2017). Mobile commerce in the United States - Statistics & Facts. Retrieved September 13, 2017, from https://www.statista.com/topics/1185/mobile-commerce/.

van der Pligt, J., Zeelenberg, M., van Dijk, W. W., de Vries, N. K., & Richard, R. (1997). Affect, Attitudes and Decisions: Let's Be More Specific. *European Review of Social Psychology, 8*(1), 33–66.

Verhagen, T., Vonkeman, C., Feldberg, F., & Verhagen, P. (2014). Present it like it is here: Creating local presence to improve online product experiences. *Computers in Human Behavior, 39*, 270–280.

Warr, A., & Chi, E. H. (2013). Swipe Vs. Scroll: Web Page Switching on Mobile Browsers. *Proceedings of the SIGCHI Conference on Human Factors in Computing Systems - CHI '13*, 2171.

Zajonc, R. B. (1980). Feeling and thinking: Preferences need no inferences. *American Psychologist, 35*(2), 151–175.

Appendix

Measurement scales in online experiment.

Goal
- In the process of choosing your preferred mug, was your goal rather targeted search or casual browsing? *(Binary choice)*

Perceived Enjoyment (Cronbach's α = .91; scale based on Koufaris, 2002; Jiang and Benbasat, 2007)
1. I find my experience with this website interesting.
2. I find my experience with this website enjoyable.
3. I find my experience with this website exciting.
4. I find my experience with this website fun.

Perceived Diagnosticity (Cronbach's α = .89; scale based on Jiang and Benbasat, 2005; 2007)
1. This website is helpful to me to evaluate the product.
2. This website is helpful in familiarizing me with the product.
3. This website is helpful for me to understand the characteristics of the product.

Attitudes toward Shopping at the Website (Cronbach's α = .94; scale based on Grazioli and Jarvenpaa, 2000; Coyle and Thorson, 2001)
1. I like shopping on this website.
2. Shopping on this website is a good idea.
3. Shopping on this website is appealing.

Intentions to Return (Cronbach's α = .92; scale based on Coyle and Thorson, 2001)
1. Next time I need to shop for a mug, I would like to use this website.
2. Next time I need to shop for a mug as a gift for a friend, I would like to use a website with characteristics similar to those of this website.
3. I would use websites with similar characteristics to those of this website in the future.

VI   Overall Conclusion

In this final section, we provide a concise summary of the key findings from our four articles. Then, we outline the most relevant managerial implications and close with a discussion of avenues for future research.

Our first article shows that the topic of product experience through digital touch is primarily addressed by marketing literature. However, our results indicate rising interest from the disciplines of management, information systems, and psychology. Furthermore, we observe that while studies in the early 2000s emphasized on software-enabled interaction through visual and functional control mechanisms, more recent research has shifted the focus toward hardware enablers such as touchscreens. Moreover, we find that studies in the fields of marketing and psychology concentrate on laboratory experiments to understand underlying mental mechanisms. In contrast, field experiments and empirical datasets that observe actual consumer behavior are mainly used in management and information systems research.

From our second article, we draw three main contributions. First, we define concrete, quantifiable dimensions of UX and identify associated disciplines. Second, we propose a formalism named QUX to measure these dimensions via a survey that companies can use to obtain feedback from their customers. Third, we develop a corresponding tool which helps to visualize the survey results and improves communications across departments and within interdisciplinary teams. In summary, QUX links existing UX evaluation methods in a structured way and provides a starting point for future work towards a more commonly shared understanding of UX in industrial practice.

The results of our third article facilitate the understanding of virtual product experience in computer-mediated environments in several ways. First, we contribute to the literature of visual control mechanisms and show that alternative photo technology leads to decreased product interest but higher willingness to pay, while zoom technology has no similar effects. Furthermore, we demonstrate that these effects of visual control mechanisms are substantially different on touch-based mobile devices compared to non-touch PC interfaces. Finally, we establish textural fit as an important driver of object valuation on touch devices.

Our fourth article contains three main findings. First, we demonstrate that goal orientation moderates the relationship between consumer perceptions and attitudes. More specifically, browsers are primarily driven by enjoyment and searchers by diagnosticity. Second, we find that assortment size negatively moderates the (otherwise positive) relationship between screen layout and perceived enjoyment. Third, we discover that consumer attitudes toward certain combinations of UI elements are substantially different depending on goal orientation.

The articles presented in this dissertation hold several managerial implications. With regard to a product's user experience, we learned from expert interviews that product development processes and respective UX paradigms differ substantially from one company to another. For example, early-stage startups might share a much more holistic view on their product and UX, but lack structured processes. For these companies, our quantified user experience (QUX) approach could provide meaningful guidelines. Moreover, with companies increasing in size and operating in maturing industry sectors, the number of involved disciplines, departments, and stakeholders is steadily rising. In these cases, QUX could enable more efficient communications. Concerning mobile user interfaces, we conclude that marketers should be aware of the complex interplay between different types of visual control, product-specific characteristics of their offerings, and their customers' primary touch points across device types. Most importantly, we demonstrate that interactive technologies can have opposite effects on touch and non-touch devices. Hence, it might be advantageous to enable certain visual control mechanisms for touch devices only. Furthermore, we show that alternative photo technology increases consumers' willingness to pay – such ways of dynamic product presentation could be of relevance in shopping environments that delegate pricing power to consumers. As regards the consumer perspective, our findings on goal orientation provide a further step into the direction of disentangling the complexity of user-centered interface design. We find that there is no single superior design solution that would fit everybody at any time. However, since goal orientation for every individual consumer is situation-dependent, we suggest that mobile UI design should not only adapt to technological restrictions such as smaller screens, but also to the behavioral needs of individual consumers.

Besides theoretical and managerial implications, there are several data-, method-, and technology-related challenges that provide avenues for future research.

From a data-related point of view, we find that across our four articles, most of the related studies in the fields of management, marketing, information systems and psychology were conducted in laboratory settings. While the underlying survey data generates valuable insights into latent psychological mechanisms, there is still a lack of large-scale observational datasets that enable more insights into real-life purchasing behavior. Particularly valuable conclusions could be drawn from field experiments that track users within closed online shopping ecosystems across devices and for a longer period of time. Furthermore, we find a positive effect of visual control mechanisms on consumers' willingness to pay in our third article. Against this background, it might be interesting to study online retailers who delegating price-setting to consumers.

From a methodological point of view, one of the main challenges when researching the effects of virtual control mechanisms and digital touch is to control for product-brand awareness. Whenever consumers had exposure to commercials or a well-known brand prior to data collection, results might be biased due to different, unobserved levels of product-related uncertainty.

This becomes particularly important when researching visual control mechanisms that influence consumer decisions through increased product information – hence, brand-related effects should be considered to gain a better understanding of product-level uncertainty and its effect on purchase decisions. Another challenge, related to the digital interface, is to measure unbiased effects of variations in virtual control mechanisms per se. During experiments both in the field and in the lab, it can be difficult to isolate, e.g., control- or gesture-specific interaction effects which can be attributed to a particular presentation format.

From a technological point of view, major challenges come with rapid advancements on both the hardware and the software side since many of the latest interactive technologies and dynamic presentation formats require certain minimum standards regarding data volume, bandwidth, and processing power. Thus, they might not be accessible to a large part of customers relying on mobile technology from previous device generations. While researchers must find ways to account for heterogeneous device capabilities in the field, retailers face the challenge of ensuring backward compatibility. From a software perspective, a large number of augmented and virtual reality applications will become viable in the near future and provide more opportunities to create multisensory product experiences. Virtual reality technology in particular could enable substantially higher levels of immersion and real-time interaction. From a hardware perspective, an increasing number of computer-mediated interfaces is equipped with sensor technology that allows for multi-touch gestures as well as adaptive interface design based on the user's emotional state. In summary, such technological advancements create many new opportunities for virtual product experiences on touch-based mobile devices.

Revisiting the two quotes by Bill Moggridge cited in the introduction, it has become apparent through the course of our four studies that mobile devices play an important role in bringing digital and physical interaction closer together. Modern interaction design for touch-based smartphones and tablets creates multisensory product experiences and adapts to individual consumer goals and needs. Looking at the bigger picture, this dissertation shows that the topic of designing for interaction on mobile devices is an emerging literature stream which could and should be addressed from various angles. Both the exploration and recombination of product-, interface-, and consumer-related factors hold a large variety of opportunities for future research. In conclusion, we hope that the overall results of this dissertation encourage more interdisciplinary work in academia and practice alike.